KT-170-252

Steve Biddulph has been a psychologist for thirty years. He was one of the pioneers of family therapy in Australia, working with struggling families in the industrial city of Launceston, where he recognised that there was a need for books that were humorous, easy to read and matched the needs of young parents without much time or energy at the end of a busy day.

His first book *The Secret of Happy Children* certainly filled this niche, reaching over a million parents in 27 languages; it has been in print for 20 years. Steve has also worked with sexual assault victims, Vietnam Veterans, the police, emergency services and, for eight years, directed the Collinsvale Centre, which taught medical professionals to use counselling skills and understand people's feelings as well as their bodies.

In 1994 he released *Raising Boys* - a number one bestseller in countries as diverse as New Zealand and Brazil. *Raising Boys* broke the logjam of thinking about nature or nurture, detailing how by working with nature – boys' physical and hormonal differences - we could then nurture them into caring, safe, exuberant and focused young men.

Biddulph was voted Father of the Year in Australia for his contribution to encouraging fathers to engage with their children. He visits the UK, Germany, Japan, New Zealand and Korea regularly to work with parents and also in encouraging school systems to be more boy-friendly. All proceeds from Steve's talks and seminars are used to improve Australia's treatment of refugee children and their parents and for the care of refugee families across the globe.

Manhood

Steve Biddulph

Vermilion
LONDON

1 3 5 7 9 10 8 6 4 2

Copyright © 1994, 1996, 1998, 1999, 2000, 2002, 2004 Steve Biddulph and
Sharon Biddulph

Steve Biddulph has asserted his moral right to be identified as the author of
this work in accordance with the Copyright, Design and Patents Act 1988.

All rights reserved. No part of this publication may be reproduced, stored in a
retrieval system, or transmitted in any form by means electronic,
mechanical, photocopying, recording or otherwise, without the prior
permission of the copyright owner.

First published in Australia in 1994 by Finch Publishing Pty Limited
First published in the United Kingdom in 1998 by Hawthorn Press
For further information on Hawthorn Press titles see www.hawthornpress.com

This edition published in the United Kingdom in 2004 by Vermilion
an imprint of Ebury Press, Random House UK Ltd
Random House, 20 Vauxhall Bridge Road, London SW1V 2SA

Random House Australia (Pty) Limited
20 Alfred Street, Milsons Point, Sydney, New South Wales 2061, Australia

Random House New Zealand Limited
18 Poland Road, Glenfield, Auckland 10, New Zealand

Random House (Pty) Limited
Endulini, 5A Jubilee Road, Parktown 2193, South Africa

Random House UK Limited Reg. No. 954009
www.randomhouse.co.uk
Papers used by Vermilion are natural, recyclable products made from wood
grown in sustainable forests.

A CIP catalogue record is available for this book from the British Library.

ISBN: 0091894816

Printed and bound in Great Britain by
Bookmarque Ltd, Croydon, Surrey

Contents

Acknowledgements

I would like to remember the late George Biddulph whose sense of adventure brought our family to Australia from Yorkshire almost fifty years ago and, even in his dying, helped me with my life.

And to thank my school teachers, who often were fantastic men and women who gave so much to a child of dubious potential.

Rex Finch at Finch Publishing, for risk taking and hard work. Martin Large at Hawthorn Press, for championing this book in the UK, and graciously allowing this new edition with Random House. Julia Kellaway, Trish Burgess and Amanda Hemmings for teaching me to speak English. Ian and Veronica Ochiltree for organising my tours with idealism and good heart. Doro Marden and everyone at Parent Network. Colin Fowler and everyone in Northern Ireland Parent Advice Centres and the Male Link. My teachers, both Christian and Buddhist, for the tools to live in a broken world. Shaaron Biddulph for helping me join the human race. My son for his open heart and strong conviction. My daughter, for the laughter and challenges.

Permissions

Grateful acknowledgement is made to the following people and organisations for permission to include their material in this book.

All quoted matter by Robert Bly in this book, unles otherwise stated, is taken from his book, *Iron John*. This material is reproduced with the kind permission of the publishers, Element Books of Shaftesbury, Dorset, UK.

'Male Bashing', which first appeared in *To Be A Man*, K. Thompson (editor), is reproduced with the kind permission of the author, Fredric Hayward, MR Inc., PO Box 163180, Sacramento, California 95816, USA.

The interview with Charles Perkins is extracted from 'The Return to the Dreamtime', with the permission of the author, Mr Stuart Rintoul, and the *Australian* newspaper.

The cartoon, 'Trouble at the I'm OK, You're OK Corral', is reprinted with kind permission of The Cartoonist Limited, London. The cartoon, 'The Demon', is reprinted from *A Bunch of Poesy*, by Michael Leunig, with the kind permission of Collins/Angus & Robertson Publishers, a division of HarperCollins Publishers Australia.

Sources for brief quotations are given in the bibliography. Where other quotations have been used, every reasonable effort has been made to seek permission and include full accreditation of the source prior to publication.

Foreword to the UK Edition

I'm standing backstage at Melbourne's Concert Hall, and my heart is threatening to beat right out of my chest. I don't usually get stage fright before a talk, but sometimes it just hits me out of the blue, so I use a tried and true remedy – I go and chat with some of the audience waiting in the lobby. This nearly always works because it reassures my 'inner child' that they are a friendly bunch, eager to have a good time.

I've been out in the lobby for just a few minutes when I notice a big, bearded, tattooed man in a denim shirt with the sleeves torn off standing not far away. He's noticed me too, and he beckons to two other men he is with. The three of them begin to move across and in a moment he is right there, his head tilted back and a frown on his face.

'You been following me around?'

My mouth opens and shuts wordlessly, but I am thinking, 'Help!'

He doesn't let me suffer long. His face breaks into a wide grin. 'That bloody book of yours – that's the story of my bloody life, mate.' I grin too, as I slowly work it out, and soon he is introducing his father and brother. He explains, while they silently nod in agreement, that the three of them had been estranged for years until he had read this book *Manhood*, and passed it on to the other two, and they had 'sorted things out' between them. They had come along together to say 'thanks' in person and see what else I had to say.

For a family psychologist, job satisfaction doesn't come much better than this, and yet it's a recurring message. A week or two earlier I had heard something very similar from one of Australia's few truly philanthropic billionaires, so it had nothing to do with class or education. *Manhood* was doing what I hoped – given men a tool they could use to break out of their isolation and outdated macho roles. The idea was catching on: you could be a real man and still be warm, open and live a free and exuberant life. There was more to life as a man than just being a 'walking wallet'.

Manhood was first published in Australia, then Germany, and was read by half a million people across Australasia, the UK and Western Europe in its first year of release. The USA had *Iron John* by Robert Bly and *Fire in the Belly* by Sam Keen, both excellent books, but *Manhood* spoke more to regular, hard-headed men, and looked to more earthy and lasting changes. What *Manhood* said was that there is more to life as a man than lonely struggle, earning and spending, being a cog in an industrial society you don't even like. It also said that men's conditioning – in family, school and popular culture – was seriously handicapping us and it was time for a change. (Remember, there was something called Women's Liberation that did just this for women, with remarkable success, several decades ago – so it was not impossible.)

The book was part of a broader discussion just starting to break out. Hundreds of magazine articles, newspaper columns, radio debates and thousands of conversations were taking place about the possibility of men changing, not (like good little boys) because they *should* (a famously unsuccessful formula for change) but because they were beginning to find that they *could* and wanted to. Movies such as *The Full Monty* and *About a Boy* were addressing the question of masculine choice, and even the hit TV show *Seachange* had a men's group. Awkwardly, hesitantly, something was starting to change.

Women's liberation, for all its successes, has not been enough to bring the needed changes. There are bigger issues than who does the housework or who is the chair of HSBC. We are still a civilisation going to hell in a handbasket of materialistic greed. Our current almost hysterical obsession with terrorism seems rather ingenuous, given that our relationship with the undeveloped world is almost entirely one of theft. Fair trade, debt reduction, no longer propping up vicious regimes because they are someone we can do business with are the only real solutions to the eternal risk of terrorism. The danger to our children's children is not terror, but corporate globalised waste and consumption, driven by the unhappiness of Western men, and women too. We have to change ourselves fundamentally if the world is going to work. Everything is connected. How you make a living, what you consume, how you spend your time – the questions of men's liberation – will determine the future of the globe.

There is great confusion right now about where we are going. Social trends swirl about, like the currents at the change of the tide. Yet it's always like this when a significant change is beginning. It's getting better even as it's getting worse. While some men work 60-hour weeks, others are quitting their jobs or cutting their hours to have time to love their children. While some men think money is God, others are simplifying and walking away from wealth, choosing freedom of time to be creative or involved in their community. While some men are drowning their sadness in drugs, drink and promiscuity, others are rediscovering the joy of intimate sex, friendliness and compassion in their relationships with women. Men are starting to change.

If you have just started reading this book, I hope you will find it makes a difference in your life. If you like it, please share it with friends and talk about the ideas in it. Your yearning to be happier and your efforts to find a larger life are part of the world's salvation too.

Steve Biddulph
Launceston, Tasmania
January 2004

Chapter 1

The
Problem

Most men today don't have a life. What they have instead is an act. When a man is deeply unhappy, desperately worried, or utterly lonely or confused, he will often pretend the opposite, and so no one will know. Early in life little boys learn – from their parents, from school and from the big world outside – that they have to pretend. And most will do this for the rest of their lives.

The act that a man puts on is drawn from a very small range of choices, clichés almost: he may play the role of tough guy, family man, hard-nosed businessman, detached professional, cool young dude, and so on. The core pretence of all these roles is that 'everything is fine'. What's more, every man seems to believe that if he just keeps up this pretence of happiness, it will magically one day become true. But it rarely does. Thoreau puts it best: 'The mass of men lead lives of quiet desperation.' And he's right. At the end most men lie on their deathbed with a look of bewilderment and failure; that something more was supposed to happen, but didn't. Many of us have sat beside these deathbeds and witnessed this bewilderment. It's tragic and a waste.

Most women today are not like this. More and more, women live from inner feeling and spirit. They have their problems and struggles, but most women today have a clear sense of self, and they relate to at least several friends and family members with almost complete honesty. Women generally know *who they are* and *what they want*. The men in relationships with these strong and healthy women are simply no match for them, in every sense of that word. Conversations go nowhere and relationships collapse because to be in a relationship you have first to know who you are, and the man does not have this worked out.

Acting happy when we are not places us in terrible emotional isolation. When a man kills himself, or does something else precipitate and harmful, friends will often declare, quite truthfully, 'I had no idea...' The pretended life also damages our families, which often consist of a woman and children who are close, with a man standing off to the side, unconnected and anxious. It is also the reason there are so few authentically vibrant men to lead us. We need a Nelson Mandela, but we get a Tony Blair. We need a Martin Luther King, but we get the Archbishop of Canterbury. It's because of the long-running man-crisis that we are in such a mess within our families, as a nation and in the world as a whole. Yet the solution is not all that hard to find. As a society, we have only gone half way. We have liberated our women (who, with their ability to collaborate and verbalise problems, were easier to liberate anyway), but we have done nothing comparable for our men. So it's time something was done.

How the difference began

How did this difference between men and women come about? It seems important to understand this if we are to undo the tangle and start again.

Little children start out well enough. A young child, whether they are a boy or a girl, bounces into life as if it were a spring garden. They expect to find every day an adventure and a pleasure. But early on, a difference starts to set in, and you can see this in your own family. A boy's spirit begins to shrivel. By mid-primary school he is uptight and edgy, and by the teenage years he is in anguish. (Sue Townsend's clever but deeply fatalistic books about Adrian Mole treat this course of events as normal, yet it is essentially a blighting of adolescence, a case of development thwarted and stunted by a lack of real adult help. The adults in Adrian's life are incompetent, self-seeking and lost.)

What becomes clear to us as we examine the lives of

boys and men is that key ingredients for growing up well are simply not provided to boys in our culture, and have not been for hundreds of years. By the time the twentieth-century boy became a grown man, he was like a tiger raised in a zoo – confused and numb, with huge energies untapped. He felt that there must be more to life, *but he did not know what that 'more' was.* Lacking any idea how it might be different, he just worked harder at the pretence. Alcohol, drugs, compulsive sex, workaholism, sports could distract or numb him, but they didn't provide answers. They didn't provide any real sense of freedom.

Pretending is hard work, so it's not surprising that eventually a few cracks start to appear in a man's façade. Even a moment of joy can be the trigger for this. Sometimes a man gets a fleeting glimpse of being fully alive. He finds himself alone on a beach or mountain-top and suddenly feels dissolved in the waves, trees and sky: he regains a sense of being connected to the natural world. Or in a certain kind of moment with a woman – of intense passion or the sudden sweetness of compassionate understanding – he understands fleetingly what it really means to be close to another human being. Or playing with his children, he suddenly feels like a child again, loses all self-consciousness, feels laughter coursing through his body. In these moments he glimpses some-thing unsettling but beautiful...and then it passes. He almost feels worse off, not knowing how to get that moment back, so he shuts the memory away and goes back to business as usual.

More often, the breakdown in a man's act can occur in more painful ways – marriage problems, a child taking drugs, business or career failure, a foolish traffic accident. Or, in the middle years of life, a deep despair combined with exhaustion settles upon him as he realises that not only is he not *loved* by those closest to him, but he is not even *known* by them. His connection to his own life suddenly appears to be the thinnest of threads, ready to snap at any moment. We hear such stories every day.

Not long ago, I was addressing a seminar of school principals. It was the first session of the morning. The group was strangely quiet, so much so that in the end I asked if something was wrong. They told me that just before I had come in, they had learned that one of their colleagues, a man in his thirties with two young children, had drowned himself. They were not completely surprised. His wife had rejected him sexually and begun an affair with another man. This was bad enough, but as it became public knowledge, it had proved too much to bear. The man had been great at his job, much loved by parents and children at his school. Everyone was devastated. They loved him, and now he was dead.

When writing this book, I began to remember instances of male disintegration running right back through my life. A good friend of mine in high school had been intensely driven to do well. In the final exams he managed five distinctions out of six subjects –a superb score, but not a perfect one. On the night before taking his place at university, he waited until his family were all asleep, then went out on the riverbank behind his home and killed himself. Sometimes even the prospect of becoming a man is too much to contemplate.

What is important here is not the adverse situation these men found themselves in, for marriage problems or career setbacks are very common, almost universal. The problem is that both these men, although much loved by their friends, did not feel able to share their problems, so their friends did not get a chance to show they cared.

There is clear evidence (see page 13) that all through the twentieth century men have been suffering uniquely and severely from problems of unhappiness. Not just suicide, but premature death from stress, accidents, violence and addiction – the statistics are all dominated by men. And hurt men tend to hurt others. Physical violence against spouses, sexual abuse of children, divorce, moral bankruptcy in business and politics...all point to something badly wrong with large numbers of men. As Robert Bly puts it, 'Are you depressed enough already?'

Reconnecting men

The bad news helps us to know where to begin. The biggest breakthrough in health research over the last decade has been not in wonder drugs or technology, but

Facing the facts

We are often told it's a man's world, but the statistics on men's health, happiness and survival show this is a lie. Here are some of the *facts* about being a man in the twenty-first century....

♦ Men, on average, live for six years less than women do.

♦ Men routinely fail at close relationships. (Half of all marriages break down, and divorces are initiated by the woman in four out of five cases.)

♦ Over 90 per cent of convicted acts of violence will be carried out by men, and 70 per cent of the victims will be men.

♦ In school, around 90 per cent of children with behaviour problems are boys and over 80 per cent of children with learning problems are also boys.

♦ Men comprise over 90 per cent of inmates of gaols.

♦ Men are also 70 per cent of the unemployed. (A million men have disappeared from the workforce in the last decade, while two million more women have joined it.)

♦ Men and boys commit suicide three times more frequently than women. (Twice as many men kill themselves as die in car accidents. *Five thousand men in the UK take their own lives each year – or about 18 per day.*)

in understanding the effect of social support – specifically on recovery from cancer and heart disease and, of course, on depression and mental health. People with friendship networks, intimacy, laughter and play in their lives have better immune systems, more energy, clearer thinking, are less prone to panic or extreme acts, and less likely to get sick or die. We are soothed and healed when we have a supporting net of social connections. Women usually have this, but men usually do not.

When we compare the longevity of men and women in Britain today, we find a stunning difference. In health terms, men are like a Third World country. Just pause for a moment and make a guess at what is the biggest killer of men in the developed world. It's not heart disease or cancer or traffic accidents. These deliver the final blow, but they are not the cause of death. Most men die, years prematurely, from the 'big L' – loneliness. Men live in the same society as women, but they do not connect to it in the same way. As a result, they do not gain its benefits. And this difference kills them.

This has to change – and we should start changing it now – with our baby sons, with little boys in school, with teenagers, and with adult men. Men's liberation has to be the next great social project. Without men of integrity and wholeness, how can a society hope to survive?

The rest of this book is a road map to show how this is done. My purpose here has been to make a point – that malfunctioning men are not the exception, but the rule.

The whole way we 'do' maleness has come unstuck. Today's modern urban or suburban man is a pale imitation of what being a man can be. In Shakespeare's time, even in Dickens' time, in other cultures, times and places, men had just so much more 'juice'. Here in Britain we have the longest history of industrialised urban living in the whole world. We are, in a sense, the most 'tamed' men on the planet. And therein lies the problem.

Today, at long last, we are questioning the roles that have been handed out to us: cannon fodder, factory fodder, office fodder, divorce fodder. We've had enough of malfunctioning role models: politicians we can't trust, grey men in suits wrecking our world, idiot sportsmen and boring drunks. There is a sense that we can be better than this – real, alive, warm, funny and tender, intelligent, passionate, focused, gentle and strong. We are getting ready to change the meaning of manhood, starting with *ourselves*.

Chapter 2

Liberation for the Rest of Us

Sometimes the obvious can go unnoticed. About 10 years ago, writers and commentators around the world began pointing out something that we had never noticed before – that compared with the rest of the world, and compared with the rest of history, boys and young men in our society are profoundly *under-fathered* and are rarely given the processes or the mentor figures that could help their growth into mature men. With no deep training in masculinity, boys' bodies still turn into men's bodies, but they are not given the software, the inner knowledge and skills, to live in a male body with its unique hormonal and neurological traits. The result of this is an epidemic of dangerous, out of control, immature men. And that's just the politicians! Gangs, violence and uncontrollable school classrooms are the extreme effects of this father- and mentor-hunger. But even more common are the sub-clinical symptoms of this missing 'vitamin F' –

lost, depressed, conforming but essentially empty men who can't engage properly with women, children or each other, and so cannot create healthy families or communities.

It seems obvious that if you live in a man's body, you need to learn how to 'drive' one from someone who knows how to drive their own. Older cultures provided this intensively, but ours is just too busy making money to be able to do it. If you examine any pre-industrial culture, you will find that men were intensely involved in the lives of children – teaching, caring for them, handing on skills first hand. There are still remnants of this in the world today, and the skill and care involved is touching to witness. Taking children to a restaurant in Italy, for example, is a much happier experience than in the UK because the male waiters will fuss over them and enjoy their presence. In much of the Third World, men and older boys routinely nurture and care for little children with skill and interest.

An American colleague of mine was visiting Red Square in Moscow with his family. His four-year-old scampered off ahead and suddenly ran into a gang of young men coming around a corner. My friend winced with fear, but the teenagers immediately smiled at the child, picked him up, gave him a genuine cuddle and carried him back to his parents. In the more 'backward' countries of the world, people are more tender to children, they have more time for them, and more skill in teaching and helping them.

Most fathers in the developed world are distant from their children, and have been so ever since industrialisation occurred about six generations ago. Studies of how long men play or interact with their children come up with figures like six or eight minutes a day. To make matters worse, a rapid succession of hammer blows – world wars, recessions, migrations – has added to the damage. Reeling from this, most fathers in living memory have been gruff, awkward and emotionally shut down. Even modern involved fathers, making brave and good efforts to be part of their children's lives, often feel ineffectual or lacking in some innate wisdom. It's not just a playmate that growing boys need, although that's a good start. It's not just fathers they need either. There must be a whole male community, diverse and offering different ways to be a healthy male. Yet elders – the uncles and mentors of an earlier age – have all but disappeared from the scene. Once a grandfather was someone in his late forties. Now he is so old that he can hardly stand up, let alone go for long walks in the snow, discussing life's meanings and deeper joys. Unless a boy is good at sport, is in the Scouts, or encounters an outstanding schoolteacher, he may simply not know any men closely at all. Not knowing the inner world of real men, each boy is forced to base his idea of self on a thinly drawn *image* gleaned from television, cinema and his peers, which he then acts out, hoping to 'prove' he is a man. Each boy then does his best to live his life using this one-dimensional façade, which does not really work in any of life's arenas.

Girls, on the other hand, have a totally different experience. They usually grow up with continuous exposure to a range of competent and communicative women at home, at school and in friendship networks as adults. From this they learn an open and sharing style of womanhood that enables them to get close to other women and to give and receive support throughout their lives. Men's and boys' friendship networks – if they have them at all – are awkward and oblique, lacking in intimacy and often short term. (When my schooldays ended, I simply never saw any of my classmates again. Likewise when I left university and my first job.)

The lack of in-depth elder male connections during childhood leaves men bereft and struggling. Whether we are attempting to be the 'Sensitive New Man' or are clinging to the John Wayne, 1950s tough-guy image, we keep finding that it just doesn't work.

The first steps to healing

To begin with, most of us just feel there is something wrong with *us*, that we are deficient and have only ourselves to blame. But if we imagine what our life could have been like if competent, caring and wise men had always been there for us, teaching, guiding and encouraging us through our boyhood, our teens and the trials of

"You need to get in touch with the hurt child within yourself."

"I'm sensing a lot of hostility here..."

TROUBLE AT THE I'M OK, YOU'RE OK CORRAL

being a young parent, for example, and how differently our lives could have gone, then we have made a start. We can see what we might have missed and need to make up.

But it's a painful start. We feel let down, bereft, grief-struck. Yet to feel grief is a sign of progress in a man who has been shut down all his life. As a man really starts to feel what he has missed out on, he replaces the dull sense of 'lostness' with a sharp and painful sorrow. This is a positive step, *though it does not feel like one*. Change starts with acknowledging where you are – so important for us men – precisely because the denial of the pain is what keeps us in our inner prison. Toughing things out is a short-term survival technique, but not a good way of life. Continue with it, and you become numb and dead. Surprisingly, then, grief is the first sign that we are becoming alive. It also serves as a compass, since it starts us yearning for what we have lost so that we can begin the journey to recover it. It readies us to accept what we have tried to pretend we didn't need: closeness, trust, friendship, creativity. Grief is often much more fruitful than anger, which is our habitual reaction and one that has often been so destructive in our lives.

Women in the twentieth century had to overcome *restriction*, so anger was probably an appropriate response, but men's difficulties are with *isolation*. The enemies, the prisons, from which men have to escape are:

- Loneliness.

- Compulsive competition.

- Lifelong emotional timidity.

Coming out from behind these walls (slowly, carefully) will mean that men become more alive, sensing more, laughing more, responding more in body and mind – to our own benefit and to the great benefit of women and children. Only men's liberation can deliver the changes that women and children have been waiting for.

Judging by the hope and relief I encounter as I speak about these things, many people are excited about this new way of looking at men's potentialities. In Tokyo recently I spent four days talking to journalists about men's liberation. In each interview there was a point where the journalist put down their pen, forgot where they were, and began to talk about their own life: their estrangement from their father; their long work hours that kept them from their baby or child; their lack of real friendship; their longing to be more creative. The women publishers who organised these interviews would draw closer and their eyes would shine as the male journalists began to get it. The female journalists would talk sorrowfully about their husbands feeling trapped in their jobs, and go home clutching a copy of the book to show them. (Japanese men, you might like to know, are in even worse shape than their British counterparts.)

Apart from the warmth and appreciation that men show for these ideas, there are other encouragements. Mothers of teenage sons come up to me with tears in their eyes, anxious and happy that something might really happen to improve their boys' self-esteem. Wives drag their husbands along to my lectures, and it's all I can do to stop them elbowing the poor sods to death. Single women, air stewardesses, women on trains, looking for a 'real man' to relate to, urge me to get a move on.

Men are a problem to women, but rarely is this intentional. They are to an even greater degree a problem to themselves. The gender debate raged for 30 years, often fruitlessly, before we woke up to the fact that *men are not winners. There are very few happy men.* Feminism was too simplistic a model to explain what was really going on. Men and women are co-victims in a pattern of living and relating that is in drastic need of revision. Simply blaming men doesn't change a thing.

We men are a practical gender, not given to talk unless it leads to action. In the past there seemed no point in complaining, since nothing could be done. Our choices of how to be a man were so limited. *The suburban car polisher, the corporate drone, the sexually incompetent 'new lad' – some choice!* For men, the shift had to come 'back to front'. Only with the possibility of change can we finally admit how bad it really has been.

This is the end of the theoretical part of this book. Seven aspects of men's lives are tackled in specific detail in the chapters that follow, and practical action is suggested that you can begin today. Most, if not all, of these seven aspects will have immediate resonance for you, and one or two of them may be positively life-changing. Good luck.

Other voices
....

Who *taught* us to be a man? Nobody!

Marvin Allen, *In the Company of Men*

We are living at an important and fruitful moment now, for it is clear to men that the images of adult manhood given by popular culture are worn out; a man can no longer depend on them. By the time a man is 35, he knows that the images of the right man, the tough man, the true man, which he received in high school, do not work in life. Such a man is open to new visions of what a man is or could be.

Robert Bly, author of *Iron John*

It is nothing like the women's movement, and probably never will be. Each man seems to be struggling with it quietly – at 25, or 35...men are at the edge of a momentous change in their very identity as men, going beyond the change catalysed by the women's movement. It is a deceptively quiet movement, a shifting in direction, a saying 'no' to old patterns, a searching for new values, a struggling with basic questions that each man seems to be dealing with alone.

Betty Friedan, *Second Stage*

Make no mistake about it: women want a men's movement. We are literally dying for it... We have to use our instincts when deciding what to trust. We need to ask questions... Then women can find allies in this struggle for a future that has never been.

Gloria Steinem, in *Women Respond to the Men's Movement*

Chapter 3

Seven Steps to Manhood

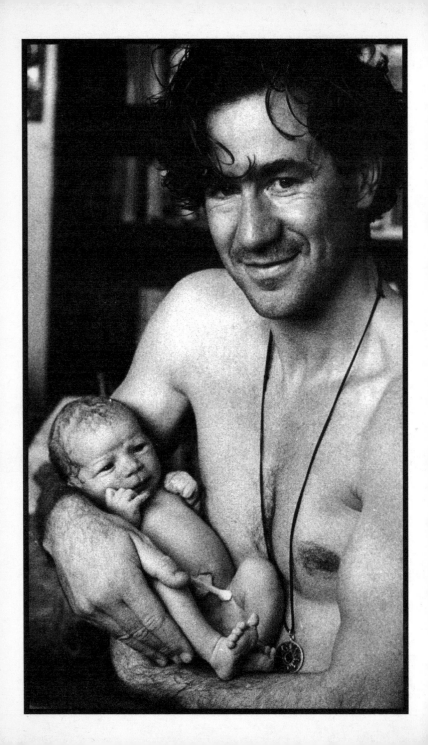

Let's start with a simple question to you as a man. Are you happy? Or are you just pretending to be and hoping that pretending will one day make it true? Do not answer this too quickly.

Left alone, a seedling will grow into a tree and a tadpole will turn into a frog. But a human child does not turn into a functioning adult without lots of help. To learn to be the gender you are, you probably need thousands of hours of interaction with older, more mentally equipped members *of your own gender*. We are all human, and we can learn a huge amount from parents and carers of either sex. But we can never be complete without deep involvement with adults of our own sex. Imagine if a girl was raised by men alone, in a monastery, say, or with a single father, and all her teachers and carers were male – we would have real concerns for her development into a woman. Yet this same-sex deprivation is the normal experience of millions of boys.

In our society, girls get deep contact from women on a day-to-day basis, but boys rarely get it from men. Women raise girls and boys, and most primary school teachers are female. Most of the day, most of the time, men are usually not around in the lives of children. The result of this lack of male contact is a problem we are all aware of: in today's world, little boys often just grow into *bigger* little boys. They become emotional children in adult bodies. The loneliness of this and the confusion – not knowing how to be comfortable with normal masculine feelings or how to be close to other males – just makes the pretending more compulsive and more isolating. *The loneliness of men is something women rarely understand.*

It takes the help of many men to turn a boy into a man. School doesn't do it. Watching television doesn't do it. Mum, however hard she tries, can't do it on her own. Boys need exposure to healthy men, and this need continues into adult life. Young men need older men and middle-aged men still need even older men. If this need is met, life becomes vastly more bearable, secure, interesting and friendly. The sense of lonely struggle and imminent failure is replaced with an experience of life as a supported journey to mastery.

The reason it has taken so long to find this out is that we don't miss what we don't know about. If your developmental needs were not met in childhood and adolescence, you wouldn't necessarily know this. Even children growing up in the most bizarre families assume that their life is normal. You will only get a suspicion that things are amiss when your life starts to go wrong. This is what is happening to men today. Problems with health, marriage, parenthood, the ability to make friends and failure at work are some of the ways they are alerted to the deep holes in their being. As young men we act cocky and cheerful, but as the pressures of life stack up, our deficiencies become more obvious. The abysmal performance of our male leaders at all levels of society is a symptom of this problem. A male leader needs to draw on exceptional fathering experiences since he is father to a team, an organisation or even a country. He needs to draw on a deep experience of emotional intelligence and wisdom in each and every situation that life presents.

In nature, all development follows a pre-determined sequence. In a man's development, the sequence has been forgotten and the process left largely to chance. If we look at older cultures, we see immense and focused efforts going into the raising of boys: rituals, teachings and processes that have only feeble equivalents in our culture.

Robert Bly and others have identified a number of missing steps in men's development, which we'll explore shortly. Perhaps these steps are the keys to really having a life as a man. The aim is not just to be well adjusted but to be something more worthy – to have a glorious and well-rounded life. Without idealising the past, we can still observe that the Sioux hunter, the Masai herdsman, the

Aboriginal elder and the medieval craftsman lived glorious and multi-dimensional lives – creative, sensual, spirited and integrated around the care and protection both of their people and of the natural world. Why should today's man have to be any less a man than his ancestors?

The steps to manhood

The steps to full development as a man are clear and specific. They are not always easy or quick, but they offer a blueprint that is an enormous improvement over simply muddling on. Rather than unfold these gradually, let us hit you with them first up. Reading them in this way may just touch a chord that gets you thinking. We can look at the details later. Here goes...

Step 1: 'Fixing it' with your father

Your father is your emotional line of contact to your masculinity. You have to work towards a clear and resolved relationship between yourself and him. *You cannot get on with your life successfully until you have understood him, forgiven him and come in some way to respect him.* You may do this in conversation with him if he's alive, or in your mind if he is now dead. Unless you do this work, his corpse will drag around behind you and trip you up every time you make a move.

Step 2: Finding sacredness in your sexuality

You have to find out how to be not just comfortable but transformed and fulfilled in your sexuality. Sex will either be a sleazy and obsessive part of your life, or a sacred and powerful source of well-being. There isn't any in between. First you must relocate your sexual energy in yourself instead of giving it away to women. Then you need to learn the art of courtship – the specific role a man must take in the dance of male and female.

Step 3: Meeting your partner on equal terms

Anyone can start a relationship – the trick is sustaining one. To do this you must learn how to meet your partner, and, in fact, all women, as different but equal beings. This means respecting her but respecting yourself too. In order to have a successful marriage and one that lasts, you will sometimes need to be able to debate fiercely and to do so in a safe and focused way so that problems get solved. In a modern marriage, soft men are boring, yet bullies drive self-respecting women away. Today's man has to learn both to communicate his own feelings, and listen to those of his partner. This takes great balance.

Step 4: Engaging actively with your kids

You can't parent from behind a newspaper, and you can't leave it all to your partner either, because it isn't fair, and because a woman doesn't have all the ingredients needed. You will have to get the 'tough–tender' balance right with your children. This is important for sons, for the reasons we've mentioned, and for daughters, who depend on fathers for a considerable amount of their self-esteem and their whole template for relating to the opposite sex.

Step 5: Learning to have real male friends

Being a man is almost impossibly hard at times, and to do it you will need emotional support from other men. Other men can also help you find out how to complete your own initiation into manhood. They can also provide a community of men for your teenage sons and daughters to experience, and so make up the gaps that you can't always fill. And having male friends is invigorating. They remind you to loosen up, and they deflate your ego every chance they get.

Step 6: Finding your heart in your work

You must find work you can believe in so that the time and energy of your working life are spent in a direction where your heart lies. It isn't enough just to make a living. The real work of men is to support and protect life, and to build towards a better world. If you don't believe in your own work, then the inner contradictions of it will slowly start to kill you. Since most jobs today are for heartless corporations whose goals we do not believe in, this is a huge issue.

Step 7: Freeing your wild spirit

The god of men does not dwell in the suburbs or office towers. Inner steadiness does not come from achievements or possessions. You will need to find a spiritual basis for your inner life that is specifically masculine and *based in nature*, that connects you to the earth you live on. As you grow older, this will be your source of strength and harmony, freeing you from fear and dependency on others.

That's the list. The sequence is not fixed. Some may be already accomplished in your life, others current and still others seemingly insurmountable. Some of these points may puzzle or surprise you, some may be striking a chord. By now you might be full of questions. If so, that's good. The whole of this book is devoted to exploring these ideas and to spelling out their practical implications. All of the above steps are necessary for you to progress to full manhood. So let's get started.

Other voices

··

What is a man supposed to be? What did you learn about how to be a man? From the audience, 'Big boys don't cry!' Big boys don't cry. The single most damaging thing you learn.

Marvin Allen, *In the Company of Men*

There's no sense in idealising pre-industrial culture, yet we know that today many fathers now work 30 or 50 miles from the house, and by the time they return at night the children are often in bed, and they themselves are too tired to do active fathering.

Robert Bly, *Iron John*

A man needs other men – especially older men – to bless him, to honor him, to encourage him, to point out his mistakes and to raise his status.

Douglas Gillette, *The Lover Within*

Chapter 4

You and Your Father

When I meet with men in gatherings around the world, I often conduct a survey. It has only one question: 'How do you get along with your dad?' The results are always the same. Around 30 per cent of men report that they don't even speak to their father. Their relationship is non-existent. Around another 30 per cent have a somewhat 'prickly' or difficult relationship. They do sometimes spend time with their father, but it's painful and awkward; visits turn into arguments, conversations into stand-offs. Around another 30 per cent of men fare somewhat better. They visit their father or phone him regularly, show up for family get-togethers, go through the motions of being a good son, yet discuss nothing deeper than lawnmowers. The relationship is involved, but it is boring and dry. It is kept up mostly out of duty and does not nourish or sustain. Finally, there is a group of men who are different to all of the above. These men smile, and their eyes shine when they speak about their father. They say things like, 'My father is great. He's a friend, but much more than a friend. He's an emotional anchor in my life.' This group, however, is tiny. *Less than 10 per cent of men are friends with their father.* What a terrible statistic this is. How tragic that we all don't have this kind of relationship, and the sense of ease and quiet pride that comes from knowing 'my father loves me and is proud of me'. How different the world would be if we all – men and women – could count on this.

Where are you at with your father? And with older men in general? These are important questions: your happiness as a man is hugely impacted by the answers. Manhood, it turns out, isn't an age or a stage – it's a connection both to the world of women and of men. Half of this equation isn't enough. Unless you can connect to the inherited masculinity of generations of older men, you are like a phone without a socket. Thousands of years of masculine culture is missing for you.

Think about this connection with your father for a moment. Your masculinity – unconsciously and whether you like it or not – is based on his. Most men realise (with alarm) that their father's mannerisms, stances, attitudes and words are deeply a part of them and likely to emerge at any time. If you are at war with him in your head, you are at war with masculinity itself. And this, in turn, often means you are hopelessly divided against yourself. This is not to say you should be like your father. But the differentiation has to be made consciously, with awareness and through dialogue, and not out of blind reaction.

Without understanding our fathers and knowing them well, we cannot decide what we want to take and what we want to leave of their legacy.

It's important at some stage of your life, if you possibly can organise it, to have a profound conversation or series of conversations with your father. Only by doing this can you get an understanding of his life, his reasons, his failures and his successes. Unless you take this step, you will always be building your own manhood on shifting sands – on guesswork and childhood impressions that were never the whole story. Other older men and women may supplement what you didn't get from your father – and their role is vital – but his primary place in your life will still be there. Even if he was an alcoholic, a wife beater, a child abuser, even if you never met him, your biological father still matters. Until you come to terms with him, he will haunt you from the inside, where he symbolically lives forever.

How your father colours your life

One of the ways your father will 'hang around' is by colouring your attitude to all older men. Perhaps you don't trust older men because you couldn't trust your father. Perhaps you are rebellious to authority in general because your father was unloving and harsh. Perhaps you try to impress older men because you couldn't please your father. Perhaps you have been feeling superior to older men, that you can do without them, or can get one over them. The fact is, until you reach a place where you can feel love and respect for your father and also *receive* the love and respect of older men, *you will remain a boy*.

I have spoken to men whose fathers died or abandoned their families and were never seen again. I've talked to many men whose fathers committed suicide. This leads to deeply buried hurt and confusion, since the message a little child always takes is, 'What did I do to make him leave? What's wrong with me?'

Men can suppress this pain by hard work and denial, but will still be prone to outbursts of deep distress, often masked by anger. I've encouraged such men to make the journey into their father's past, which often means making a real-life journey back to their birthplace or across the globe. It has led men I've known to visit prisoner-of-war camps in Japan, to talk to contemporaries of their father, to look up long-lost relatives, to make a deep personal journey to heal the emptiness and understand the whole picture and so let themselves and their fathers 'off the hook'. The journey can be into your own memory bank as long-forgotten incidents and experiences surface. Listening to other men's stories helps to trigger this, since our childhoods might have been alike.

Sometimes dreams bring new information, or long-lost

memories will surface. As a young man in my thirties, I was very focused on the deficiencies of my father, the things he didn't do or offer me, especially during my adolescence. Naturally, my psychology training fed into this – parent-blaming being a major industry at the time. One evening I was watching a video that my partner had brought home, thinking it might interest me. The movie was about a father and son with a tempestuous relationship; at one point in the story they had a fist fight beside a busy highway. As the movie ended, I suddenly began to cry – something I had scarcely ever done since childhood. It was not just quiet weeping either, but huge gulping sobs. I was suddenly remembering specific positive things my father had done when I was very young. Keeping me warm inside his coat at a soccer game, bathing my sores when I awoke in pain and distress with chickenpox, holding my hand as we walked out on snowy nights when I was about six years old. I had blocked out these memories because they didn't match the story in my head that my dad was never close. The real story was so much more complex, rich and valuable.

Coming to terms with your father, having a rounded view of him, is especially important if you are a father yourself, and more so if you are in any kind of leadership role.

For those of us whose fathers are still alive, the situation is easier – somewhat. Many men will identify with this story of a man phoning his father, long distance. The younger man is making an attempt to bridge the gap that has grown between them. Father and son have had little contact in recent years, and the son has been doing some thinking. When the father answers the phone, the son begins to try to tell him...

'Hi, Dad, it's me.'

'Oh, uh huh! Hi, son! I'll go get your mother...'

'No, don't get Mum. It's *you* I want to talk to...'

[Pause.]

'Why? Do you need money?'

'No, I don't need money.'

[The younger man starts on his somewhat rehearsed, but still vulnerable speech.]

'I've just been remembering a lot about you, Dad, and the things you did for me. Working all those years in a job you hated to put me through college, supporting us. My life is going well now and it's because of what you did to get me started. I just thought about it and realised I'd never really said thanks.

[Silence from the father. The son continues.]

'I want to tell you...thanks. And that I love you.'

[Long pause before the father answers.]

'You been drinking?'

Whenever I tell this story the audience laughs out loud, but the men laugh with eyes wet and shining.

What fathers wait to hear

Every father, however much he puts on a critical or indifferent exterior, will spend his life waiting at some deep level to know that his son loves *and* respects him. Make sure you absorb this point. *He will spend his life waiting.* This is the huge power you hold in your hands, just by virtue of being a son. Everyone these days accepts that a parent has the power to crush a child's self-esteem. Few realise that a child, eventually, holds the same power in reverse. Parents wait, however defensively, for their children to pass judgement. That's how life is.

A friend of mine had a father who simply walked out of the house if ever somebody tried to talk to him about something that made him uncomfortable. The old man eventually developed cancer and was dying in hospital, with tubes in and out of him. My friend went to the hospital, closed the door of his father's room and said, 'I've got you now!' He began to tell him how angry he was and also (after a time) what he appreciated about him. At the end they were holding hands.

At one stage in my life, I drove my father to a remote beach and refused to take him home until we talked. He came through very well.

So there is a responsibility here – and not just a duty.

Getting this right will challenge you to the core. The words 'I love you' are cheap and easily said, which is part of the reason we hesitate to speak them. It's not the words that matter. But the message is important, however it is conveyed. Whether it is through a tone of respect, a liking for each other's company, a hug or a touch, you will find your own way. Eventually though, to remove any doubt, you have to tell your father (and your mother) what you feel and all that you feel, or else just go on fudging it.

A lot is at stake. If you are a man and you do not confront this dragon, your father will die hurting and a part of you will die as well. Robert Bly claims, *'Many men go to their graves convinced that they have been an inadequate human being.'* They do this because of the lack of respect that has developed with those they love – not the least of these being their sons, their connection with eternal masculine life.

So please don't leave it too late. It is possible that your father will seek you out one day to deal with this himself. It is possible but unlikely. You are the one who has the benefit of the insights of our generation. You are the one reading this book. You are the one who has grown bigger by standing on his shoulders. It might be up to you to make the first move.

Finding your father

You may have in-built prejudices against your father, for a surprising reason. Very often and sometimes with the best of intentions, a mother will turn her son against his father. Robert Bly has a brief and powerful story (in the video lecture 'A Gathering of Men') which, when he tells it, lands in an audience like an emotional hand-grenade. It's about a man who decides to make up his own mind about his father:

> At about 35, he began to wonder who his father really was. He hadn't seen his father in about 10 years. He flew out to Seattle, where his father was living, knocked on the door and when his father opened the door, said, 'I want you to understand one thing. I don't accept my mother's view of you any longer.'
>
> What happened?
>
> The father broke down into tears and said, 'Now I can die.'
>
> Fathers wait. What else can they do?

If you're a father with an adult son and reading this book, why wait? If you're a son with a living father, then Bly's challenge is clear. Are you ready to make that journey? Often, to start with, you don't feel much love for your father, much less respect him. Perhaps you hate him. If there are differences between you, then these cannot be ignored. *Don't pretend things are OK.* It simply won't work and you will feel cheapened. Differences have to be dealt with (more on this later). As Robert Bly has observed:

> Some father-hungry sons embody a secret despair they do not even mention to women. Without actually investigating their own personal father, and why he is as he is, they fall into a fearful hopelessness, having fully accepted the generic diminished idea of father. I am the son of defective male material, and I'll probably be the same as he is.

Finding an understanding of their father's position is necessary for all sons if they are ever to graduate as men. *Respect (love mixed with admiration) is the food of the male soul.* Sons have to 'discover' respect *for* their fathers, which is not the same as pretending it. They also need to receive respect *from* their fathers.

The approval all sons crave

In a superb Christian book on men's development, called *Healing the Masculine Soul*, Gordon Dalbey, a minister, tells the following story.

A young man in his late twenties writes to his father. The young man is a successful professional, but plagued with insecurities and hurt by the difficult times he had with his father through his teens. In his letter he is direct and to the point. He asks his father whether he loves him. A letter comes back in reply, courteous and formal in tone: 'I love all my kids – you should know that.' Can you spot the deliberate error?

The young man feels let down, though it takes a while to work out why. He eventually realises he's been short-changed and *this was what always happened*, throughout his childhood. 'I love all my kids...' A clear statement is deferred, left to implication. Direct praise is avoided. Direct contact is never made. Encouraged by Dalbey, the son persists. He writes again. He is frightened to do so, but he takes a chance. Here are the exact words of the father's reply:

> I have to thank you for pushing me with your question. I guess I hadn't really thought that deeply about it. But when I did think about it, I realised that I do love you, Peter, and I need to say that for myself probably as much as you may need to hear it.

Nothing is more powerful in the psychology of childhood than the need for love and approval. Unless a child receives clear and tangible demonstrations of these, then he or she will wither like a flower without water. It's as basic as that. I've watched tiny children in hovels in Calcutta dancing for their family and friends, who respond with warm applause and hugs. I've also watched

British children bring home report cards from their expensive public school, young faces eager for praise, only to receive cool, critical appraisals from their performance-orientated, uptight parents.

I don't in my heart understand where this parental coldness comes from. When I look at my own kids through certain eyes, the urge to hug them and praise them to the skies is sometimes overwhelming – not because they are different from any other child (or just because they are 'mine'), but because they are young human beings and glorious. Something must go badly wrong for parents to shut down these natural feelings.

What is the result of lack of closeness with the father? If love is what we hunger for and it is not forthcoming, then a warp in our life sets in. When our natural need for love is fulfilled, it settles into the background and we can get on with our life. Unfulfilled, the need for approval drives us like an obsession. Many of the people who dominate our media – business tycoons, politicians and obsessive sports achievers – are mostly driven by this unfulfilled hunger. '*See, Dad? See what I can do?*' And, of course, it doesn't work. '*But, son, can't you do better?*'

There are many possible causes for a generational rift between fathers and sons. While it is always difficult for men of differing generations to reconcile with one another, especially in times of rapid social change, consider the problems raised if there is a major difference of orientation – for instance a gay son (or a gay father for that matter). At heart the issue is really the same: 'Do you love me, even though I differ from what you expect? I am not the one you dreamed of.' The movie *The Sum of Us*, with Jack Thompson and Russell Crowe, is great viewing for any father, however young their son might be, as a way to relax around this issue.

Expectations and hopes are part of the psyche of every parent. It's equally important to let go of these should they not work out. Many terrible wounds arise in families from fathers who wanted a son and got a daughter; wanted an athlete and got an artist; wanted a musician and got a labourer; wanted Olympic gold and got cerebral palsy. The problem is not the different outcome but the refusal to grieve and then move on – to love what you have got instead of what you wanted.

It might be one of the biggest stretches imaginable for our souls – to abandon our shallow, egotistical dreams and to realise how much better our real children are than any dream could be.

Fixing it with your father

Clearly, things are best worked out between living fathers and sons. Once you accept this as a necessary step in your own liberation, it comes down to practicalities. Men I talk to often say they avoid starting any real discussion with their fathers for fear of starting a huge fight – of making matters worse. 'He's too old to change now,' they say. 'It's better to let things be.' Perhaps many fathers also live in fear that their sons will show up armed with sacks full of blame and criticism of their inadequacy. They are hardly likely to expect a good outcome.

One solution is to go in with an open mind. Don't start with your fists up – 'Justify yourself, you old bastard!' – wait for the right time. Go for a drive or a walk. Be somewhere private, not a café or bar. Be sure to get him away from your mother; he will feel a need to protect her or withhold the truth if she is close by. Ask him for the true story of his life and how it was for him during your childhood. Ask him about his work, his life and the decisions he made. Be non-judgemental. (If you find it hard to be this way, remember that your son will weigh you on these same scales.) Try to have no agenda other than understanding. Your father may well be suspicious, waiting for you to spring the trap. Unless you can be really open, you may not get the real story.

Go back further still. Find out what was going on in your father's childhood. Then move on to when he was raising you. The truth – his truth – will often be quite different from your childhood impressions. You are humanising your father in your own mind by doing this, filling out the picture, letting him off the hook of the role all children cast their parents in.

Some fathers will be totally evasive, walking from the room, refusing point blank to speak. I've known fist fights to develop, but I don't recommend this. Remember the goal: you are breaking down *the defences*, not the man. Take it slowly. Some men take their father away camping or fishing for a few days so that things can develop.

A friend of mine in Germany had always known that his father had survived something terrible during World War II. All he knew was that his father had been about 11 when Russian soldiers came to their village; he had never spoken of what happened. He had always been a remote, tense man, though deeply caring for his children. They now lived hundreds of miles apart, and saw each other only once or twice a year. My friend asked his father for help in redecorating his apartment, knowing the father would make the long journey to help. (The apartment was actually not so bad as all that.) They painted and worked for five days. On the last day, the father finally began to talk about the war. What he recounted having witnessed was horrific (there is no need to recount it here). As he spoke, he began to weep, and the son turned to him and put his arms around him. The old man needed his son to understand what he had been through, what had made him so tense all those years. He was finally ready to do this. It happened because my friend created the time and the place, and was patient, so the two of them could find peace.

The problems between fathers and sons can sometimes be very simple, not traumatic at all. Trevor, an engineer in his early fifties, gave this example. When he was a boy, his father would take him on a paper round by car every morning. They spent about two hours together each day in a peaceful rhythm of teamwork, as the sun slowly came up and melted the frost. It was his favourite time of the day; he loved the closeness to his father and the feeling of being useful in a man's world. Then one day his father was offered a chance to leave his day job (which he hated) and be a partner in the newsagency that owned the paper round. To his son's dismay, he turned it down. The newsagency business was sold and the paper round ended.

Trevor stayed angry about this for nearly 30 years. 'He doesn't want to be with me!' When his dad got old and sick, Trevor asked him about it.

'How come you didn't buy into the newsagency and keep up the paper round?'

'Because the partner was a gambler and we would have all gone broke.'

Simple as that.

Becoming a parent yourself is often the experience that prompts more compassion for your own parents, as well as a desire to be closer to them. Somehow you realise that while they got some of the fine details wrong, the sheer volume of physical sacrifice and care they took of you overwhelms this. As you change your hundredth nappy and clean up your thousandth toddler meal, you realise 'Someone did this for me too.'

A man in one of my groups, Mark, a police sergeant, supported his wife through a cancer scare that lasted about two years. At times he would be very uptight and worried, and he would often react angrily to his young son, who was just being a normal demanding kid. Mark and his wife did not want their son to know the danger she was in, and the eight-year-old was living in an unknown space – a kind of emotional minefield.

Eventually, when his son was 10, Mark joined a men's group. The other men urged him to tell his son what had happened. His son – who earlier would perhaps have been very worried – was relieved to understand, and proud to be trusted. His behaviour and school work both improved. He felt closer to his father through experiencing this trust and the apology that went with it. Children often do not know what is going on, and we don't always know how much to share with them. So we need to make corrections and changes of direction from time to time. If we don't update them, *they might just conclude that we don't like them, and keep that conclusion for life*.

As *you* talk to *your* father, you may find that many things fall into place. One of the biggest steps is to simply say, 'Thanks.' There may be many specific memories or instances that you recall as a beautiful part of your growing up. Meanwhile, your father may have no idea that he ever 'got it right'.

Some families, on the other hand, maintain a kind of family lie that they were always happy and got on just fine. Which, of course, no family ever really does. This can lead a child not to trust or listen to their inner signals.

When things feel bad, but no one is saying 'This feels bad', you begin to live a double life. For some men it is important to tell their father what they hated, what they found terrifying, or how lonely and sad they felt through his lack of appreciation and warmth. But do this with great care, not in a vindictive way, but calmly, in the overall context of the positives he also did. Be prepared for him to rail back at you. He might hear only the negatives, and feel terribly rejected, so it's important to hold both things as true – there was good, but it wasn't *all* good.

When we enter a dialogue like this we are vulnerable, but it's only in this vulnerability that real trust and connection can occur. A vulnerable space is a sacred space, where we open our hearts and others open theirs. The risk is worth it. Eventually, some understanding – some forgiveness, perhaps apology, or some new perspective – will enter into the air between you. No one can predict or program how this will happen. Prepare to be surprised.

Remember that the goal is to *get things right between you*. You are not there to get even, to 'make him suffer like he made me suffer' or anything like that. That would just spin the wheels of pain around one more time. You are aiming for a resolution that is real and complete. You want to heal both of you before it is too late.

Loving your father in yourself

Most men find talking about their father an uncomfortable subject, and men have succeeded in avoiding it for
many generations. This is a pity, because in doing so they
cut their own roots. Therapeutic lore tells us we have to
make peace with our parents, but ancient tradition takes
a less compromising approach. In a sense, you *are* your
father. You are an individual only to the extent that you
build your own structure on top of what he and the men
he descended from have given you. Deep down inside you
stand on all kinds of foundations that you must get to
know, allow for and understand. A long line of men going
back into ancient history sent their learning and their
behaviour down into your father and on to you. It's a little
eerie to contemplate, and yet it's something to be proud
of. These men survived, they raised their families successfully, they kept life going.

As noted earlier, most of us have discovered, uneasily,
that we have gestures, mannerisms or ways of doing things
that are exactly those of our father. The answer isn't to
try to eradicate them. The psyche throws nothing away.
You have to learn to love 'your father in you'. If you don't
deal with this, you will very often be at war with yourself.

How many men do you know who are like this? As
they dig the garden or fix the car, or write a cheque, you
can almost hear them muttering in argument with a long-
dead ghost: 'You're making a mess of that, son!' 'Fuck off,

Dad!' Forgiving your father – not just by effort of will but by actual understanding of his life – will be one of the most freeing things you ever do.

Some men get very sad at this point because their father is already dead, and the conversations we are suggesting can never take place. It seems that an opportunity has been lost forever. Not true. He is *in* you and you can begin the process. In imagination, in dreaming, by talking to his gravestone or writing him a letter, you can begin to shift the grief. It is awkward but important. You can go on an actual, personal odyssey – finding out more information, travelling to his place of birth and the locations of significant events in his life, talking to his contemporaries, starting to fill in the missing details. It often helps to discuss this quest with other men on similar journeys. We all have so much in common and can help to release each other's grief, finding support and clarification at the same time. A surprising amount of feeling flows out with this process, and much health and strength flows in to take its place.

Don't run from the past; it is always, eventually, a treasure trove.

In a nutshell

♦ Your father is the person who first and most powerfully 'taught' you what manhood means. He did this just by being your father. Like it or not, he is in your head and in your sinews and nerves forever.

♦ This fatherly 'inheritance' is a mixture of utter garbage and priceless treasure. Unless you get in and sort it out, you will never know which is which. Most men stay out of the 'attic', the part of their mind where this is all stored. They decide it is all junk, but leave it right where it is – unexamined. As a result, a funny smell is always drifting down and tainting their lives. At the same time they feel deprived, missing out on the jewels and riches concealed in the heap.

♦ By far the easiest way to sort the heap is to have a certain kind of conversation or series of conversations with your father. Find out from him:

• The truth about your childhood.

What was happening for him when you were conceived, born and were growing up? This will shed much new light on what was going on, perceived by you only through a child's eyes at the time.

• The truth about his childhood.

What was the story of his childhood and young manhood? What did *he* bring to bear on his raising of you?

These conversations will be a two-way exchange of gifts, as you tell him your experience and ask him questions about his. Be prepared for surprises. Don't be fobbed off with comfortable replies, clichés or skimming over things. You are after the real blood, sweat and tears of his life and yours.

♦ If your father is dead, you might have to 'dig him up'. Here are some ways:

• Write a letter to him as if he were alive.

• Visit the significant places in his life.

• Talk to others who might know more about him.

• Decide to dream about him.

• Talk with a male counsellor about him in order to reactivate your feelings and recollections.

Good luck and courage.

Other voices

··

We were not like father and son, my father
sometimes said, we were like buddies. I think my
father actually believed this. I never did. I did not
want to be his buddy; I wanted to be his son. What
passed between us as masculine banter exhausted
and appalled me.

James Baldwin, US novelist

I do not want my children to have a monolithic
memory of me... On the contrary, I would like them
to know the vulnerable man that I am, as vulnerable
as they and perhaps more so.

**Georges Simenon, creator of the
Maigret novels**

Not all men missed out. Some tell stories of
generous supporting fathers, who praised, loved
and protected them as best they could, and even
initiated them as best they could...

Robert Bly, in _Wingspan_

There's a lot of talk about physically and/or emotionally absent dads, but sons are also beginning to ask themselves, 'Was my father really absent, or did he and I unconsciously conspire to ignore each other?'

Christopher Harding, in *Wingspan*

Chapter 5

Sex and
Spirit

Sexuality, at its best, is like a doorway to paradise. It opens into places of laughter and delight, tenderness and exhilaration. It is a huge energy source. It motivates us to communicate with that most difficult and challenging feature of our world – the opposite sex. It releases us from the ordinary and allows us to glimpse wild nature, alive and free and living in our own body.

That's at its best. Sadly, though, for most men sex is none of these things at all. For many it is a source of much misery, frustration and despair. But it doesn't have to be so.

The so-called sexual revolution of the 1960s had some remarkable and positive effects, but these were not evenly handed out. For women there was a fundamental shift in self-knowledge and sexual openness. Countless books, workshops, discussions and programmes helped women to get in touch with their bodies, to honour their sexuality, and from that knowledge to confidently communicate their needs and wishes to their partners. Women learnt that they could initiate, control and choose the manner of lovemaking. And there was for a time a sense of reverence towards women's sexuality. However, many wise women commenting on this phenomenon today point out that young women are still in deep trouble because the revolution was only partial, that in fact it was hijacked by darker forces of commercial greed, as well as, let's face it, our own immaturity. Many young people today think that sex is just something like ice cream, or a 'need' with no more depth or soul attached to it than going to the bathroom. Worse still, the media and advertising agencies have annexed the message of sexual liberation for their own uses so that there is now a relentless pressure even on pre-teen girls to see themselves in terms of how they look and how sexually available they are – that this is their 'booty', their power and their only source of worth.

For men it is even worse. They might have enjoyed the sexual revolution – there was more sex going on, or at least going on more openly. But nothing in any of this served to break men out of their self-image as simply being sex machines who wanted as much sex as possible, with as many partners as possible, and with as little involvement as possible.

The shame continues

In the past, boys grew up receiving no real training in

relationships, and in fact getting all kinds of demeaning or negative messages about their deepest feelings. Today most men are basically still ashamed of their sexual feelings: they consider themselves to be essentially creeps. They are poorly developed as communicators, not really aware of their own inner world. As a consequence of this, they make love solely from the lizard part of their brain, which might satisfy a female lizard, but isn't enough for a thinking, feeling woman. The result is poor communication and, before long, a growing conflict over sex. It has become almost universal that men and women's sexual relationships reach a point of breakdown. Married couples who in other dimensions of their life can cooperate, share and trust quite well still have a miserable time in the bedroom. Only those with great wisdom, patience and a generous sense of humour manage to navigate these shoals into a happy and amicable old age.

Unequal desire develops; coldness and rejection set in. Instead of sexuality being integrated into the whole of life, its difficulties or its absence come to dominate a man's every waking moment so that most men under the age of 50 operate more like sex addicts than true lovers – needy, unsatisfied and obsessed. Sexual misery haunts our world like a vast epidemic.

Thankfully, in recent years, something new has begun to happen. Spontaneously in countries around the globe, stimulated by books like this one and those by Robert Bly and Sam Keen among others, thousands of men's groups have formed. These groups have a guiding ethos of speaking honestly, from the heart (instead of the usual locker-room posing that passes for male sharing). For the first time we are discovering how men really feel as opposed to the image-making they formerly practised with each other. As a consequence, men have begun to understand their sexuality beyond the crass and demeaning stereotype that 'men want just one thing.' This self-exploration is bringing to light many surprises and insights.

Whole new approaches to marital therapy are being developed based on this honesty, such as that described by David Schnarch in his book *Passionate Marriage*. Schnarch insists that we humans experience sex primarily in terms of its *meaning*, not just its biological functioning. Is she making love to me out of warmth? Lust? Pity? Am I pursuing her out of greed? Tenderness? Dependency? Equality?

Only by understanding what sex means to us, and bringing this communication to the bedroom, can we have a chance of sexual joy. Making love can mean a thousand different things, and only when partners know if they are dealing with playfulness, comfort, frustration, sorrow, liking or disliking can they decide how, or even whether, to make love.

Paradoxically, as men talk more honestly to other men, they are able to begin talking more honestly to women. This has a cascading effect: the relaxation and trust that grow from being accepted and valued mean that couples are able to have more exuberant and intimate lovemaking as a result. What these men's groups and researchers have discovered, and the implications for sexual healing, will be spelt out in this chapter. The reasons for our sexual problems are largely cultural and solvable. There is great hope, and scope, for improvement, and you can begin right away.

Are most men non-orgasmic?

Male sexuality, especially the nature of the male climax, is grossly misunderstood by men – and women. Columnist Michael Ventura wrote this brilliant analysis:

> Certainly the weakest, silliest aspect of feminism, which for the most part has been an overwhelmingly beneficial movement, has been its description of male sexuality. It was a description that assumed a monolithic, mono-intentional erection; it was a description that equated the ejaculation of sperm with coming. But there are many secret passageways within an erection. As far as the question of male coming it is an immense and untried question. Ejaculation is a muscle spasm that many men often feel with virtually no sensation but the twitch of the spasm. To ejaculate is not necessarily to come. Coming involves a constellation of sensations,

physical, psychic, emotional, of virtually infinite shadings. Coming may sometimes or often occur at the moment of ejaculation, when it occurs at all. But many ejaculations for many men happen without any sensation of coming.

Until a woman understands this, she doesn't know the first thing about male sexuality. Nor do many men. There is ample evidence in face after face that, as there are women who have never come, so there are men who have often ejaculated but never come. And they likely don't know it, as many women never knew it until a few began to be vocal about such things. These men live in terrifying and baffling sexual numbness in which they try the right moves and say the right things but every climax is, literally, an anticlimax. It is no wonder that in time they have less and less connection with their own bodies, and are increasingly distant from the women they want to love.

This takes some digesting. There are, it seems, orgasms and orgasms. Norman Mailer, in his book *The Prisoner of Sex*, wrote of the difference between 'orgasms as stunted as lives, screwed as mean and fierce and squashed and cramped as the lives of men and women whose history was daily torture' and contrasted these with others 'as far away as the aria and the hunt and the devil's ice of a dive, orgasms like the collision of a truck or coming as soft as snow, arriving with the riches of a king in costume or slipping in the sneaky heat of a slide down slippery slopes'.

This represents a delightful variety. (However, there is little mention of closeness, contact or any other emotional qualities in Mailer's writings. He's still hung up on sensation, not emotion. You get the feeling that it's him and his body, with some woman along for the ride.)

There is more available than just pleasure. Older, experienced partners describe a deep connection that is the real goal of lovemaking, looking soft-eyed into one another's faces, hearts open, bodies relaxed and abandoned, gradually letting go of all defences in trust of each other and of the natural power that possesses you. The fierceness that is released when you are able to trust. As a woman friend of mine put it, 'Once you have made love, just having sex will never do.'

This isn't to say that lovemaking always has to be so intense. But it can always be a meeting of two human beings, not just (to use family therapist Carl Whitaker's phrase) 'a penis and a vagina going out on a date together'.

Loving as a whole man

The popular term for sexual climax, 'coming', is such an interesting choice of word. Who is it that is arriving? Clearly, the divinity within each partner enters the room at these times. The everyday sense of self is awed and overtaken by this feeling of being something bigger and better; the truth really, since our everyday sense of who we are is never the whole story. It's a real Van Morrison moment. The god in man meets the goddess in woman and they are taken out of space and time, knowing everything, lost in love. A Christian friend explained it as if 'we made love while God was watching'. Regaining this sense of spirit in one's sexual life takes application. Like meditation, it's simple and takes years. Yet it can be as simple and as profound as just learning to relax.

John O'Hara, in his novel *Appointment in Samarra,* has one of his characters express it this way:

> I never made love before, I just screwed. But when it happened, it was like nothing I'd ever experienced before. I think I must have blacked out for a second and all I was aware of was some kind of incredible warmth, my whole body was filled with it and I didn't want to leave her or roll away from her. I wanted to get closer to her, very close. I could feel the warmth of her body against mine, soft and gentle, and for the first time in my life I stayed in a woman's arms and fell asleep.

Paul Olson, in *Wingspan,* comments on this passage: 'What he does with that experience only time will tell. He can deny it in the morning. Or he can enter it fully and never again feel the need to run away.'

Clearly, for us to experience this kind of union (what some might call 'sacred sex') requires all kinds of readiness, timing, openness and communication, as well as just good luck. A lot of other things also have to be right. It may require years of self-examination, fighting over housework, learning to trust and becoming natural. Yet these years would be clearly well spent. We start life as tender babies and spend our whole life just regaining that absolute openness and trust.

An important and helpful ingredient for total love-making is the inclusion of nature, of letting in the signals and rhythms that the natural world sends to our cells to help tune them in. That's what romance means: it means not artificial. Even in terms such as 'the romance of sail', we are noticing a preference for the natural elements over the man-made environment. The old clichés endure because they are potent triggers. We think of romance as standing on an ocean beach watching the moon rise, of dining by candlelight, of making love on a rug by a fireside or impulsively falling to the ground together in the long grass of the dunes, laughing and pulling off each other's clothes to explore the warm skin beneath. Sex is about going back to nature, giving way to wildness – something you should never get too old for. Romance means bringing a wild heart to an erotic body, with the naked earth beneath us and the universe above.

Men and whole-body sex

Feminism gave women back the power to control their own bodies and the pleasure of fully being alive to their bodies. Women today decide for themselves whether they want sex and how they want it to be. In the daring first studies of the 1950s and earlier, fewer than 20 per cent of women were found to be orgasmic. Learning to become so, and to let their partners know their needs and desires confidently and routinely, was a very major shift.

Like the women of the Victorian era, most men don't know what they are missing. One has only to watch the reptilian grunting and grinding of the men in 'adult' movies to realise that these guys have never seen or felt a real orgasm. Like the women of the pre-1960s era, many men, too, are not yet orgasmic. What they think is an orgasm is a mere ejaculation, which is only a tiny part of the story. The key to feeling more is to place less emphasis on the outer performance or actions, and more on the inner qualities of sensory and emotional experience. Sex is active, but it's also about noticing. Just as you can eat an orange without really tasting it, sex only touches us as deeply as we let it. We men feel pretty lucky if our partner asks what we would like to do in bed. But the most magical woman is the one who asks what we would like to feel.

The columnist Barry Oakley once illustrated the difference between 'doing' sex and 'feeling' sex using two contrasting quotations. The first is by Ken Follett, from his blockbuster novel *Night over Water*:

> This was not what was supposed to happen, she
> thought weakly. He pushed her gently backwards
> on the bed and her hat fell off. 'This isn't right,'
> she said feebly. He kissed her mouth, nibbling
> her lips gently with his own. She felt his fingers
> through the fine silk of her panties…

You'll notice straight away that it's all action and adverbs.
There is nothing about feeling or inner experience. The
passage is mechanical and totally devoid of charm.

By way of comparison, Oakley quotes D. H. Lawrence,
from *Women in Love*:

> She was with Birkin, she had just come into life,
> here in the high snow, against the stars. What
> had she to do with parents and antecedents?
> She knew herself new and unbegotten, she had
> no father, no mother, no anterior connections,
> she was herself pure and silvery, she belonged
> only to the oneness with Birkin, a oneness that
> struck deeper notes, sounding into the heart of
> the universe, the heart of reality, where she had
> never existed before.

OK, it's a little over the top, but so much more alive! The
writing works from the inside out, from the real experience.
Great writing about sex is rare because this level of alive-
ness is rare. You had to have experienced what you were

writing about. But at least as the reader we can imagine it, and can therefore begin to travel down that road, towards sex that is truly mind-blowing and heart-melting.

The Lawrence quote gives no details about the sex – nothing for little boys to giggle about, since they would simply not understand. These days we inform children about the mechanics of sex. How do we let them know what the real meaning of it is? One person I know told her curious daughter that it's like the best hug you ever had, but you have to do it with the right person, in the right time and place, or it's just a mess. It takes all our poetry, music, art and a real generosity to do, and still they will have to find out for themselves.

Perhaps one thing that helps is to teach the young that sex always means something. Therapist David Schnarch asks audiences to close their eyes and remember their best ever sexual experience. (I've tried this; it's great to watch people's facial expressions.) He then asks them, 'Why was it the best?' This question elicits the meaning of the experience, and people begin to call out words such as 'passionate', 'tender', 'trusting', 'funny', 'healing', 'free', 'honest', 'athletic'. Those are the happy memories. When sex is bad – and this is worth explaining to teenagers – it's because the meaning is wrong. Sex can be routine, revenge, substitute, bored, pressured, scoring, using. It can usually go well only when the meaning is shared and understood by both lovers. Before you have sex with someone, be sure you know what they mean by it.

Self-love

Sex therapists and educators encourage masturbation as an important part of learning and maintaining healthy sexuality. In a man's life, self-pleasuring begins in the early teens, long before we establish relationships with women. On a purely physical level, the purpose of masturbation is simply to ensure that sperm are kept fresh and in healthy production. (In fact old sperm are believed by researchers to be dangerous if allowed to remain too long in the vas deferens.) Most men continue to masturbate during marriage, at those times when it isn't right or possible to make love with their partners, and most healthy and happy men will continue well into old age. Yet when asked to list their hobbies on a job application, few men ever mention it!

For men who are able to utilise their imagination and capacities for fantasy, masturbation is an exercise in sexual independence and in the development of sensuousness. By not rushing, by experimenting and finding what we like, we become more skilful and alive as lovers. A man may find that he is imagining not just the physical aspects of sex, but also the relationship, the conversation, the mood and context, and so prepares himself for relating to a real woman. On the other hand, if masturbation is furtive, rushed and shameful, or distorted by too much dependence on low-grade pornography, or if teenagers do not have the privacy or sense of permission they need, then adolescent masturbation can be a training in overfocused and tense sex, which predisposes them to premature ejaculation and generally a poor quality of lovemaking in adult life.

It's important to be leisurely, relaxed and tuned into the head-to-toe sensations of arousal to be more open to the pleasures of before and after. Self-pleasuring, for both men and women, is a kind of apprenticeship. It's here that we learn what we like so that we can communicate this to our partner. It's here that we learn to let ourselves be totally receptive – surrendering to the sensations, trusting them, allowing the whole body to receive the loving energy that becomes freely available in sexual exchange.

Protecting the magic

If we were to grow up alone on a desert island, our body would still teach us that sex is magic. But living in a grubby world compromised by smutty magazines, playground humour and unwelcome attention from older men or women, boys and young men get a sleazy, animal, dirty image of their sexual yearnings. As parents, we have to work hard to strengthen the positive and fend off the negative messages bombarding our sons. As adult men, we have to remind ourselves often that our sexuality, as it is, is wholesome and good.

One night I heard a radio interview with the publishers of a weekly picture magazine. It was the kind of publication that has huge breasts pointing out from the cover every week, and headlines such as 'Warship discovered on moon'. The editors joked about the whole culture of the magazine, the stories they got away with and what the readers will tolerate.

Listening to the interview, I often found myself smiling, but wincing at the same time. The reason for the interview was widespread criticism of a recent cover photograph showing a naked woman wearing a dog chain, which had actually prompted some new legislation to restrict display of this material in public. Most people, rightly, found this cover offensive. The interviewer asked the inevitable question: 'Does your magazine cheapen women?'

'No, not really,' the editor answered. But then he went on, laughing, 'If it demeans anyone, it's the guys who read it.' Exactly.

Finding a balance

Parents in more puritanical times tried to keep their children ignorant of sex, which caused much trauma and confusion. Sexual information has made a happier, more sane and honest world, freer of the perversions and cruelties that ran thickly under the denial of a hundred years ago.

Today's parents don't object to information – it's misinformation that angers us. We want our children to enjoy their sexuality. We want this to happen, though, in a timely way, keyed to their level of growth and maturity. Many experts have noted that exposing children to the media robs them of their childhood: it frightens and overwhelms. A child's innocence can be stolen by an abuser, but it can also be knocked around badly by an ill-timed video, too. We have to be careful, and the media need to clean up their act or face a growing parent boycott.

The biggest problem with pornography is that it is simply third rate, demoralising and gross. We need more art and beauty in erotica (such as the Japanese once used in their pillow books) to convey to our kids what is really going on inside two people in love. In my early teens I saw the movie *Coming Home*, starring Jane Fonda and Jon Voigt, which included a love scene made more special by the fact that Voigt played a wheelchair-bound Vietnam veteran. It was subtly filmed, not in any way explicit, yet it was intense and magical. I knew, at 14, that I wanted to go there.

The dark side

Cheapening sex isn't the only risk. There is a deeper danger for boys and men in the power of sex. If this energy doesn't flow in a good direction, it can sometimes go in a very bad one. There has been a justified focus in feminism on the capacity of men to hurt and harm in the sexual arena – to exploit, harass, rape and kill. This isn't a peripheral concern. Rape and child sexual abuse are horrifically widespread and do inestimable damage to millions of people's lives. Yet claiming that 'All men are bastards' isn't an explanation or a cure for this. We urgently have to explore male sexual development to find out how a healthy energy can become so badly misdirected.

The following extract was written by Jai Noa, a physically disabled man, who, in his crippled state, observed that he was quickly turning into a creep. He then made an astonishing leap from examining his own condition to noticing that in our society this process happens to all men to some extent. Almost all of us feel romantically crippled at some time. Given the media messages sent to men about sex, in the constant use of sexually posed women in advertising – the look-but-don't-touch culture – we can easily start to see our sexuality as loathsome and thus begin to incubate a desire to make women suffer in revenge. In Noa's own words:

> I use the idiom 'creep' in a very special sense. 'Creep' refers to the ashamed sexuality of most men, which is an inescapable fact of our social life and one that each of us must confront sooner or later. It is ironic that if there is an almost universal manner in which men share a common crippledness, it is in the realm of sexual expression. A creature of low self-esteem, the creep feels he cannot develop sustained intimate friendships with others. Despairing of

intersubjective [mutual] happiness, he takes the other [the woman] as an object to exploit as best he can. This is a cynical attempt to validate himself through domination. The delightful joys of erotic pleasure are turned into their opposite by a guilt-ridden quest for power. The creep, then, is a voyeur, a pornophile and an exhibitionist. He enjoys not only invading the sexual space of others, but also a feeling that his penis has the power to cause a reaction, even if only one of discomfort or disgust. The heterosexual male creep tries to reduce all women to whores, i.e. to what he thinks of as dirty sluts, who are so low they would fuck someone as contemptible as himself (and thereby elevate him). He may cruise bars or parties in search of a drunken easy lay. In his masturbation fantasies he chooses a woman who is too good for him and envisions her as a slave of sexual passion.

The creep is a man who fails to live up to the romantic ideal and who feels crushed, bitter and resigned to this failure. And since most men suffer defeat in the romantic meritocracy at one time or another, the cripple can find his identity partially located in the world of men. Increasingly, during his teenage years and for an indefinite period of time thereafter, the cripple can find a bond with any men who indulge in misogyny.

Noa's insights here are ground-breaking, and of enormous consequence. When I first read his essay 'The Cripple and the Man', I sat for a long time in silence. It's possible that Noa has answered one of the social problems of our time. Let's go back to that key sentence: 'Despairing of inter-subjective happiness, he takes the other as an object to exploit as best he can.' In other words, despairing of ever winning anyone's love and closeness on an equal footing, feeling the unbearable shame of rejection, the man who becomes a creep chooses to take the upper hand. Here we can look into the soul of the rapist, the child molester, the pornography addict, the serial killer and the wife beater.

We also have Everyman, struggling to feel OK about his wants and desires in a seeming one-down position with women, knowing well the feelings expressed in the old Dr Hook song, 'Girls can get it any time they want'. This is more than just a problem of sexual confidence. Many men confuse sexual rejection with outright rejection of themselves and their lovability, so feel double the pain. (It may spread to other aspects of their performance – their earning capacity, physique, and so on.) The worldwide prostitution industry, with all its tragic ramifications, depends on this male inadequacy that our culture creates.

> *A creep has abandoned the difficult path of intimacy for the safer one of exploitation.*

All human beings need to feel loved: to be valued as

we are, treated with kindness, and to experience intimacy and affirmation as sexual beings. As long as we raise men with such a deep lack of inner worth, we will find them avoiding the risk of rejection as an equal and instead using their strength, their sneakiness, their money and other power plays to impose their needs. Women pay a great price for this. It's a double tragedy.

Preventing the evil side of sexuality is best done by strengthening the good. When little boys are given plenty of affection, when school-age children are given good information and boys grow up with happy and safe men around them, demonstrating respect for each other and for women and girls, the template is set for a happier sexuality. We can't leave these things to chance – positive intervention is needed to direct and shape the powerful forces of male sexuality, and to match it with thinking, feeling and choosing powers to make a healthy adult male.

Owning your arousal

There remains one last monster to wrestle. This one has always been with us, but in our society, with its constant media bombardment, it has grown into a large and many-clawed beast. Women hold such visual and tactile magic for men that it is easy to make the serious mistake of handing one's power over to them. They each become the golden woman, the goddess. From Venus de Milo to

Marilyn Monroe to Kylie Minogue, our psyche seems to need this mythical female. The ancient Greeks didn't confuse their goddesses with real women, though, so they avoided the dangers we now tend to face. Gordon Dalbey, in *Healing the Masculine Soul*, puts it like this:

> The so-called *Playboy* philosophy, for example, focuses on the enticing Playmate. The good news of the *Playboy* gospel is that the woman confers masculinity on the reader by sexually arousing him with her come-on posture. In reality, however, the reader has simply yielded his manly initiative to the woman. He has given his masculine spirit over to the goddess and, thus, lost it.

In seeing women as the holders of sexual attraction, as having power over men's desire, men actually give away their own sexual energy. We put women on a pedestal and then resent them for being there. We have to become aware that *sexual attraction lies not in the way a woman looks, but in the way we choose to look at a woman*. A man's life goes a whole lot better when he realises that he is turning himself on and that he is a mind with a penis, not the other way around.

Robert Masters' essay 'Ditching the Bewitching Myth' in *To Be a Man* observes that:

> No one arouses us. We arouse ourselves, no matter how convincingly we project such a

capacity on to another. Men are not bewitched
by women, but are bewitched by their own
hoping-to-be engorged appetites, or, more
precisely, by their unwitting animation of and
submission to such appetites, particularly those
that promise some pleasurable numbing.

Richard Rhodes explores this notion in *Making Love*:

Men say their penises have minds of their own,
but men are geniuses at avoiding responsibility.

This misconception usually begins in adolescence. The
culture of the soft-porn magazine provides a kind of schiz-
ophrenic split between the compliant, provocative
perfection of the glossy image and the awkward, human,
not-so-simple business of relating to real girls. As one
writer in *XY Magazine* put it so plaintively, 'The pictures
never loved me back.' The girlie magazine ethos tells a
young man, 'This is all you really want', yet delivers no
warmth, no faithfulness, just a wisp of pleasure and then a
long emptiness.

Facing down the stallion

Gordon Dalbey, who was quoted earlier, tells a striking
tale about freeing oneself from sexual manipulation. A
young married man comes to him for advice because a
woman at work has been seeking him out with tales of her

husband's cruelty. They are spending more and more time together and she is becoming increasingly seductive (or he is becoming attracted to her, depending where you locate the responsibility).

Dalbey explores the man's childhood and finds a pattern common to men in this situation. The man's father was considerably older than his mother, and was a remote type of man, who died while the boy was still in his early teens. The boy had always been his mother's comforter and confidant, even more so after his father's death. So by the time he entered adulthood, he had already learnt that comforting women with subtle sexual overtones was his role in life. In a nutshell, his father's abandonment and his mother's 'psychic incest' had set him up for just such a role.

Dalbey continued to counsel the man over several sessions. The man owned horses, and one morning an incident occurred that had direct bearing on his situation. A stallion, which had broken through a fence from his neighbour's property, was about to start mating with his mares. He found himself face to face with the highly excited, large black horse, armed only with a fence picket. He held his ground and herded the stallion back. Then, by a kind of osmosis, he discovered that he could also face down the young woman who was coming on to him at work. She was furious and hurt, but in the end she sought help from a woman counsellor instead. She later thanked him for not playing a game that would have harmed them both.

The psychic incest that can occur between mothers and sons is rarely talked about, yet it can do enormous damage when a mother makes her son into a husband substitute, even at just a verbal level. The melodramas some men create for themselves with affairs, conquests and love triangles lose some of their glamour when one realises that they are still trying to make it with Mummy.

Men and women naturally feel attraction to each other much of the time. Sexual feelings are a symptom of good health, of being fully alive. You can move happily in the dynamics of male and female if you know you are in charge of your own sexuality. You have 'corralled the stallion', to use Dalbey's phrase. Not castrated, just corralled, so you can take it where you want it to go. Men who have learnt this bring a kind of inner calmness to their encounters with women, which, far from being dulling, is erotic and tantalising to women in itself. Women are looking for this very capacity in a man. Someone who is capable of steady, fervent pursuit, not an oversized baby sucking the life out of them. Mills & Boon writers earn millions by acknowledging this facet of the feminine psyche – the irresistibility of a man who is willing to rein back his energy for the right time and place.

In a nutshell

♦ Don't mistake ejaculation for orgasm. Begin to explore increasing your relaxedness and awareness before, during and after lovemaking. Consider the possibility that there is vastly greater pleasure available, not from what happens on the outside, but from what you experience on the inside.

♦ Sex isn't a separate part of you. Your heart, spirit, mind and body need to be along for the ride. Sex is a spiritual practice, capable of transforming your whole outlook and refreshing your sense of glory in being alive.

♦ Deep sexual pleasure of the kind described above occurs only in a relationship with great emotional trust. This might take years to attain, but it's worth the effort.

♦ Tell your teenagers that sex always means something. Before you have sex with someone, be sure you know what it means to both of you.

♦ Masturbation is an essential and healthy part of men's sexuality throughout life. It is the way we develop appreciation of ourselves and our sensory potential, and realise that we own our own sexual energy.

♦ Exploitative pornography (as opposed to respectful erotica), prostitution, much advertising, rock videos and the like degrade men just as much as women. They imply that cheap thrills are all we want and all women offer. Don't be fooled.

♦ You have to guard against 'creepification', the temptation to choose power over women rather than the risky and vulnerable path of meeting them as equals. Once you are proud of your gender and your sexuality, you will not be afraid to risk rejection, and won't need to force or coerce women or children into sex.

♦ Women don't turn you on. You turn yourself on by the way you focus on women. Knowing this means you have a choice.

Other voices

···

Part of me lived outside my body – outside of
emotion and feeling, cynical and hard, believing
nothing, trusting nothing and no one... Somewhere
along the way...the split healed, at least in
lovemaking. It felt as if a dense, muffling
integument [skin] had been peeled away.

Instead of a compacted sensation localised in
my groin, my ears roared, my skin flushed, my eyes
dimmed, my innards loosened and flowed, and I was
one instead of two. I felt boluses of semen moving
up through the root and shaft of my penis like
Roman-candle charges, and then my entire body
exploded and I wasn't two or one, I was none and
everything. I was there and everywhere at once.

Richard Rhodes, *Making Love*

[The men she had known]...waited until dark, they
drank to get their courage up, they laid on some
perfunctory foreplay, and then they fucked, and
whatever happened for the woman happened
within that narrow range. I've got mine, now you
get yours. They didn't even work to enlarge their

own pleasure; once sheathed, they drove more or less straight to ejaculation. I'm not surprised they had trouble getting it up and keeping it there.

It's appalling that men willing to invest thought and energy in learning a sport...won't invest thought and energy in learning how to play generously at sex. On the evidence, far too many men are sexually selfish and self-centred, reverting in the intimacy of the bedroom to Mommy's darlings, taking rather than giving, not required, as girls are required from early childhood, to pay attention to needs other than their own.

Richard Rhodes, *Making Love*

If one appreciates the harmonies of strings, sunlight on a leaf, the grace of the wind, the folds of a curtain, then one can enter the garden of love at unexpected moments. Moreover, after a man or woman has fallen in love, the leaf looks better, turns of phrase have more grace, shoulders are more beautiful. When we are in love, we love the grass, and the barns, and the lightpoles, and the small main streets abandoned all night.

Robert Bly, *Iron John*

My mouth on her body, my tongue savouring her crevices, was like plunging my face into a bowl of ripe summer fruits and inhaling their mingled fragrances – peaches, apples, pears. All of her was fresh. All of her was beautiful.

Richard Rhodes, *Making Love*

Chapter 6

Men and Women

There are three things men need to understand if they are to get along with women:

1. Meeting your partner as an absolute equal; without seeking to intimidate her or being intimidated by her.

2. Knowing the essential differences in male and female sexuality and learning 'the dance of the sexes'.

3. Realising your partner is not your mother and so making it through 'the long dark night' when love doesn't happen.

Intrigued? Well, here we go.

Man as a lovable dope

There's little doubt that up until the 1950s it was easy for men to be bullies. In exchange for being willing to die in wars and work in mines and mills, society gave to men the reins of power and money. When all else failed, men were bigger and stronger than women, and violence was seen as a private matter and, in effect, tolerated. In recent times, though, we have not gained a balance of equals based on respect, but a kind of reversal. The average man has become something of a wimp. Most modern men, when faced with their wife's anger, complaints or general unhappiness, simply submit, mumble an apology and tiptoe away. If they grumble, they do so into their beards. For the most part they act conciliatory and apologise for being such dopes. 'I'm sorry, dear!' (If they accumulate enough 'frequent flee-er points' from this swallowed pride, though, they may well cash them in for an affair or a desertion – just to even the score.)

In the media, the lovable idiot has become a universal male stereotype for many decades, from Eric Sykes through Basil Fawlty to Hugh Grant. Everywhere you look around, the 'husband as a lovable dope' is an agreed-upon type.

Real life, though, doesn't work like the TV shows. The millions of men who adopt this stance find that it rarely, if ever, leads to happiness. Women with dopey husbands are not happy – they actually become *more* dissatisfied, *more* complaining. Often, without even realising why, a woman finds herself becoming a nag – for a simple reason. Deep down, women want to engage with someone as strong as them. They want to be debated with, not just agreed with. They hunger for men who can take the initiative sometimes, make some decisions, let them know when they are not making sense. It's no fun being the only adult in the house. How can a woman relax or feel safe when the man she is teamed with is so soft and weak?

In therapy I have talked to many strong, capable feminist women who tell me that they have finally found the sensitive, caring, new age man they thought they wanted and they are bored stiff! They are starting to drive slowly past building sites, wondering whether to whistle.

Men are not unaware of their failures in the relationship stakes. Whenever a group of men in their thirties and forties gathers, it soon emerges how many have been badly wounded. In therapy groups and self-help courses today, it's the men who are in tears. Whether they show their sadness openly, or put on a belligerent front, it's the same thing. They know they are failing to satisfy the woman in their life, they have failed to keep their relationships together and don't know what they have done wrong.

It's the hardest thing a man has to do – to hold this balance of being strong, but not a tyrant, soft, but not a wuss. In Holland and Australia a programme called Rock and Water is taught to schoolboys to help them avoid and prevent abuse and violence. The name is brilliant, and the method is implicit in the name. Boys learn when to hold firm (rock), and when to give in (water). In other words, when to listen and speak.

How to be equal to your wife

Although it may surprise many men to know it, women are only human. This means they are sometimes quite right and sometimes completely wrong. Most men are caught up in thinking that women are either devils or saints, and miss this simple point: women are normal, fallible human beings. So it follows that being married to one, you have to keep your head on straight. You cannot just drift along and let them decide everything about kids, holidays, houses and life in general, which some men do. Marriage is not an excuse to stop thinking. Not only can your wife be wrong, or immature, perverse, prejudiced, competitive or bloody-minded (just like you), but sometimes you and she just will see things differently. What is right for her may be wrong for you – it's as simple as that.

Being in a relationship means compromise on many things, but it starts with knowing who you are, which in turn means knowing what core principles and values you won't give up on. John Lee, in his classic book *At My Father's Wedding*, puts it like this:

> I'll compromise on where we live, where we eat, how many children we have, what movie we see, where our children will go to school, but not on

matters that jeopardise my soul. I need you to stop drinking in this house. I need the abuse to stop. I demand safety. I need to be nurtured. I need love. I need to express my anger. I need you to express yours. I need mutual respect and equality. I will not settle for less than what I know I deserve, which is health. I will not compromise my recovery to be in a relationship.

Partners in a relationship frequently misunderstand each other – and this does not decrease after years of being together. Human beings grow and change, and have to keep updating. A woman's experience of life is very different from that of a man. Our psychology, our biology, our conditioning only partially overlap. How can women understand us unless we explain ourselves to them? That doesn't mean you can't get along, but you do have to keep negotiating. Being falsely agreeable doesn't help either of you. Prepare for many long, patient debates.

When men won't fight

I have heard so many women say in frustration, 'My husband won't fight with me, he won't even discuss. He just walks away.' Perhaps the husband walks away because he doesn't want to get physical like his father used to do. Or perhaps he had a nagging mother and a weak father. He has never known a man with backbone. To have a happy marriage, a man has to be able to state his point of view, to debate, to leave aside hysteria and push on with an argument until something is resolved.

Gordon Dalbey tells of a woman who phoned him after he had counselled her husband. 'It's obvious Sam's getting stronger, speaking up for himself and letting me know how he feels,' she said. 'I know I've always wanted him to be that way...but...I guess there's a part of me that kind of enjoyed having the upper hand and being able to manipulate him into doing what I wanted. I want to be strong enough myself so that I don't do that any more.'

It's to her credit that this woman is willing to give up some of her power in order to experience a really equal relationship, based on intimacy and negotiation, not on emotional dominance.

The Guardian

There is a part of every healthy person's internal repertoire that we could call the Guardian. The Guardian does not harm others, that is not its purpose. The Guardian 'guards the walls' of your emotional castle and protects you from mistreatment or abuse. The Guardian is not strong in children, which is why they need our protection.

When I work with sexually abused people, a pivotal step in the healing is to help them tap into the self-protective rage that is buried inside them – a physical and emotional fury that will simply not allow harm to happen without a deadly fight. People who have access to their inner rage are awe-inspiring. They have never breathed so deeply, yelled so loud, focused so clearly. Once this capacity has been awakened, I know they will be vastly less likely to be harmed or exploited again. Only when the Guardian is mobilised can a man or woman begin to establish close relationships. In fact, only then can life really proceed. A woman will feel more able and willing to bear a child as she knows she has the capacity to protect it. (I have known fertility problems to disappear through this work – as if a woman's body would not bear a child until her mind knew it could keep it safe.)

For a marriage to thrive, both partners need to bring their Guardians along for the ride. It's not that the other person wishes them harm, just that people getting close will inevitably overstep the other's boundaries and need to be reminded. Often it's enough to say, 'Hey, you are crowding me', 'Don't make my mind up for me' or 'Let me choose my own sweater'. Sometimes things get heated. Sometimes no amount of gentle talk is enough to root out fixed attitudes or longer-term misunderstandings and pull them into the light of day.

We made a mistake during the 1950s when we pursued the harmonious, sweet and loving ideal of marriage. The passionate, heated, Mediterranean-style marriage has more going for it. The psychologist Carl Jung said, 'American marriages are the saddest in the whole world because the man does all his fighting at the office.'

The trick is to fight consciously, carefully. You can be passionate and still choose your words thoughtfully. So often, though, when men and women are fighting nose to nose, the man doesn't actually know what he wants. All he wants is for the fighting to stop; he might say he doesn't like fighting. But if he doesn't stay in this furnace, how can he and his partner ever burn off the misunderstanding and create something new and better? Perhaps the man never saw his parents fight productively. Or perhaps they were vicious, out of control, and he wants none of that. He takes every word of complaint or criticism as a spear to the heart, when, from the woman's point of view, she's just throwing mud pies. A man will collapse, or he will go off and sulk, when what is needed is just to stand there, listen and, if you see it differently, say so. There is a middle way through all this.

Fighting in marriage

Great learning and growth can come from fighting within marriage. The German writer Marie-Louise von Franz tells a story about a woman who had several marriages that were extremely turbulent and painful. They always started well, but in each one the arguing eventually led to physical fighting and then to divorce.

The friend's fourth husband was different. The very first time the wife 'threw a fit' (her words) and began to be wildly abusive, the man simply walked quietly to his room

Passion needs rules

It's paradoxical that we can only let our feelings flow freely, and only be truly passionate, when we have certain boundaries laid down. Trust has to be there, but the boundaries mean:

- Never being violent or even threatening to hit or harm.

- Never walking out of the house mid-fight (though you can walk out of the room – see below).

- Not using put-down language. No name-calling, no disrespect, no sarcasm (these are often women's weapons, and she must be strong in relinquishing them).

- Staying on the point and not bringing in other material from long ago or other topics.

- Listening to the other's point of view while honouring your own.

- Taking time out by agreement, if it becomes too heated, to think it over, and returning to continue the argument. (Time out is especially important if you feel you might become violent or irrational. The early warning signs are not hard to spot. Simply say, 'I need to cool off right now, this is too heated for me' and go to another room.)

These rules allow you to debate cleanly and respectfully until understanding is reached.

and began packing his things. He refused to fight 'dirty', as was being expected. His words were beautiful: 'I know I am supposed to act like a man now and shout and hit you, but I am not that sort of man. I will not allow anyone to talk to me in the way you have, and I am leaving.' The woman was so shocked that she apologised. The couple are still together.

It's important to point out that if the woman in this story had been making a point, asking for a change, then the man needed to stay put and listen. But this was quite different. She was simply 'having a fit'.

Men and women have had huge problems in the centuries since industrialisation, which handed down a great legacy of abuse, betrayal and hurt (see page 138 for more about this). It's possible that we can carry in us not only our own accumulated rage and sorrow but also that of our mothers, fathers and grandparents. Under stress couples may simply drop into a blind and unthinking anger that does huge harm to their ability ever to trust again. Two friends of mine, both health professionals, have a loving relationship and a strong religious commitment to their marriage. Yet both are deeply frightened on the inside because of their childhood histories of violence and mistrust. At times when they disagree, neither seems able to stop a spiralling escalation of screaming, threats, physical blows, and one or both taking their things and driving off into the night. It's horrific for them and for their young children, who listen to all of this from the bedroom and wonder if someone is going to get killed.

What can you do to end a pattern like this? Recognise the early warning signs. Learn to calm yourself through deliberate strategies of breathing, meditation and slowing down when you notice you are getting overloaded. Make a commitment to govern your own words and actions. Seek out one of the reputable therapies that heals old fears and releases the nightmares of childhood so that they don't keep flashing into your present.

Being close but different

Learning to disagree is what gets you beyond the stage of honeymoon, where, let's face it, you are essentially in love with the fantasy you paint on to your partner like a convenient canvas. Author Sam Keen puts it well: 'Romance is all "yes" and heavy breathing – an affair built around the illusion of unbroken affirmation. Marriage is "yes" and "no" and "maybe" – a relationship of trust that is steeped in the primal ambivalence of love and hate.'

'Love and hate' don't have to be all that dramatic. It's as simple as switching between 'I just want to lie with you here forever' and 'Will you, for God's sake, leave my desk as it is – I know where to find things!'

'But I was just tidying it up.'

'Well, *don't*!'

We all want to be close, but no one likes the feeling of being swamped. What therapists call 'individuation' –

becoming your own person, while staying invested and caring to each other – is a lifelong process.

Giving up violence

So far, everything we have said about the genders is equally true of both. But men and women are unequal in one important way. Usually men are bigger and stronger than their partners. And neurologically, it's been found that males react to emotion more quickly and more strongly. Learning to 'drive' a male body safely requires extra and different training from learning to be in a woman's body.

Every community needs to have training programmes for men (and sometimes for women) who wish to eliminate violence from their family situation. Here is a typical account of such a group.

In a room at a community health centre a group meets for eight weeks. There are two leaders and eight men, all of whom are there because of a history, or a fear, of violence against wives and children. As we join them, one of the leaders is talking with a man in the group, who looks awkward, his arms crossed tightly across his chest.

'Dave, you say you "roughed her up". What does "roughed her up" mean?'

'I pushed her around a bit, nothing bad.'

'How did you push her?'

'With my hand. She was swearing at me. She'd been late home from her class.'

'How hard did you push her?'

'Not very hard. She just fell back against the wall and she started to cry.'

'Did she look scared?'

'Yes.'

'So you pushed her hard enough to make her feel pretty scared of you?'

'Yes.'

'How do you feel that you made her so scared?'

'Not good.'

'Is that something you'd like to learn to handle better – that kind of situation?'

'Yes. That's why I'm here.'

'OK.'

The process, as you can see even from this small exchange, is one of becoming more honest. If you can tell the truth to yourself, what once 'just happened' becomes 'a choice I made'. By providing support for the difficulty of a man's life, understanding from others who have been there, and a complete unwillingness to allow bullshit, such programmes gradually give a man an ability to be in absolute control of himself. It's a great feeling.

In a marriage both partners have their own methods of asserting power and control. Lacking his partner's skill at using words, feeling powerless in the bigger world (unemployed, having low status or stress at work), having a history of witnessing violence as a child, a man may default to violence more easily. However, for the pattern to be broken, men must commit themselves to giving up violence as a method of control. Research tells us that only a very small number of men are psychopaths or sadists with a real wish to harm and dominate – and these men are not too hard to identify. Most men who commit domestic violence are essentially good men, who have partners who love them and do not wish to leave them. They are caught in a cycle, desperate to break out if there is an option,

Men's groups need to be led by men who have acknowledged and faced their own capacity for violence. They know the pressures a man feels in his life, and also the cop-outs and self-justifications.

Isolation also plays a large part in the problem. Many men in such groups state that before coming to the programme they have never had friends who could listen to their situations. The men they meet in the groups are, paradoxically, more confronting and more supportive than any they have met. With this kind of male friendship, they are less dependent emotionally on their wives, so there is a new relaxation and ease in their relationships. This is close to the heart of what men's liberation is all about.

Men changing men

When men build new community with each other, they can reinforce new sets of rules. 'It's wrong to hit women. It's wrong to hit children. We are your friends and that is why we tell you this. And, if need be, we will stop you with legal means if you refuse to stop yourself.'

Brotherhood of this kind means other things too. For instance, not sleeping with another man's wife – because you can understand how he would feel, and you don't want to do that. If a young woman approaches you at a bar and tells you that her husband is no good or doesn't understand her, you tell her she needs to talk it through with him. It won't help to tell *you* about it.

Which brings us around to sex.

Sex and 'the dance'

A story...

Many years ago, when I knew more than I do now, I occasionally ran weekend workshops for couples. One such weekend was with married couples from a church congregation.

They are all nice people. In fact, a bit too nice – especially the men. Good-hearted but just too agreeable. The soft slippers, neat garden, never-a-cross-word type of guy.

We are working through a list of topics and it's the Sunday afternoon, getting late. One of the topics on the list is 'Sexuality and the Dance'. We haven't got to this topic yet. A man in his late thirties, sitting on a beanbag, leaning comfortably against his sparky young wife, asks, 'When are we going to do sexuality?'

'Oh,' I say, with a grin, 'we might get round to it in a little while.' (I'm teasing him, but I don't know why.) 'It depends if there's enough time.'

'Oh, OK,' he says, and slumps back in his beanbag. My sense of mischief grows.

'Is this what he does in bed?' I ask his wife, grinning.

'Yes, it is,' she says.

She seems to know what I mean. He looks bewildered, so I elaborate.

'Well, you wanted to do something about sex. I wasn't sure. So you quit. You gave up. Don't you know you're supposed to persist? You want it handed to you on a plate?' He starts to blush, but he's not unhappy. He's catching on fast.

'You see, that's how sex works,' I go on (making it all up as I go along). 'You need to be considerate and patient, sure, but you don't give up. You have a part of you that is wild and free and just wants to go for it.' (I want to use stronger language, but it's a church group...)

'The thing you don't realise is that, treated properly, at

the right time, this is what she wants too.' (I have to stop speaking at that point because his wife, sitting alongside but not in view of him, is biting her lip and nodding 'Yes!')

Again, writer Robert Bly has put this beautifully: 'One intense sexual storm in a hay-barn means more to her than three years of tepid lovemaking. She wants passion and purpose in a man, and she carries a weighty desire in her, a passion somewhere between erotic feeling and religious intensity.'

Persist

The secret of being a suitor (which is still needed even when you have been married for half a century) is to persist – without being a pest – even if it takes weeks. Biology made women slow to burn (at least, some of the time) and men quick to explode. A skilful lover needs to damp down his fire but not let it go out. Foreplay and pursuit take place over days. Even when lovemaking has started in earnest, he holds back. Gradually, as tenderness, skill and intensity of connection set her alight, he can abandon himself more and more to his passion, catching up with her in joyous abandon. A woman friend of mine expressed it this way: 'It's power harnessed that I love, power driven and directed and held in just the right amount of check. That's the sexiest thing there is.'

Confidence

Lovemaking and courtship take more than a little confidence on the man's part. As activist Marvin Allen rather crudely put it, 'Between first meeting a gal and getting where you want to be, there are 573 chances of rejection.' In our culture we start relationships too soon. (Or perhaps we hold back the initiation into manhood too long. A century ago you were a man at 14, and expected to prove it. Today we can still be a boy at 30. This does not make for good relationships with the confident and self-aware young women of today.)

As boys, we can easily lose our sense of self in the heady perfume of our girlfriend's radiance. We can tumble head over heels into an inviting cleavage, and never find our way out. (As an 18-year-old, I spent a year of Saturdays helping a beautiful girl of my acquaintance to wash and manicure her poodle. It's not an interest I have really cultivated ever since!)

Older cultures forbade courtship until a boy had passed through significant initiation processes and was man enough to keep his sense of self. This was for the boy's own good, as much as anything. Today, if you've come through some hardships in your life, achieved some worthwhile goals, made and kept good friends, been of value to others, if you know your limitations and your strengths, you come to a woman with fascination but also with self-respect – on equal terms. You are much more likely to choose well and to find someone who wants to be a team player, rather than lead you around by your necktie. Strength attracts strength.

A space of your own

Many men have no space of their own in the house. Clearly, from the decor and furnishings, the bedroom is usually the woman's space. If a man goes to work, deals all day with pressures and then comes home to more pressures, there isn't anywhere that he can just be. Along with having a room of one's own goes time of one's own. Setting aside time each day to be yourself and do your thinking means you have a more equal footing in the household and less need to stay overlong at the office or the pub.

Use your space to gain a sense of self. Early in the morning, or before bed, take time to find yourself again. Move in a rhythm out and in again, so that when you are with your children, your partner or friends, you are really with them, not distracted or mentally absent. And when you are alone, be alone.

Also use space to be with your partner in a quality way. Go round the corner with her to a restaurant or park so that you can have 'couple time'. Use the physical world – beaches, forests, the busyness of the high street – to express the different states of mind that you want to encompass, the different aspects of yourself.

Getting through the long dark night

Most of us get together with a woman first and then grow up second – if we're lucky and she is patient. So it's likely that some crises of growth will occur, which we will have to find our way through within the relationship. There is one outstandingly common crisis, which is probably behind 90 per cent of marriage break-ups (however much other reasons are cited). You could call this stage 'the long dark night'. It would be more edifying if it were 'the long dark night of the soul', but it's really just the long dark night of the penis. Let me explain.

We fall in love mostly by good luck. It just happens. Maintaining love is often left to luck, too. Unlike those cultures where marriages are arranged, ours doesn't recognise that love is a craft that takes practice. Eventually, most men and women lose the spark – they fall out of love as quickly as they fell in.

The man usually denies this to himself and is happy enough as long as his partner stays sexually available. It may be that, for men, sex has a kind of sedating, reward-at-the-end-of-the-day quality (as expressed in that popular song 'Morning Train' by Sheena Easton). Sex is a compensation for the treadmill quality of the rest of life – with a mortgage, young children and retirement still decades away.

Very often, though, a woman tires of routine sex. (Or with young children, or perhaps a job, she is just plain tired.) The very thing that makes a man a good husband

– his devotion to being a stable provider – wears out his spirit and makes him boring. Finding sex and marriage unrewarding, she starts to cool down. She exerts her right not to make love. The man sulks, suffers, grouches and schemes, to no avail.

For a man with inner resources, this is only a temporary setback. He admits in the first place that sex *was* actually routine, that the relationship had gone hollow – and perhaps he was not as content as he had been telling himself. He begins the concerted work to get things restarted: planning holidays or weekends together; relieving her of the pressures of children; cutting back his work commitments so as to be more energetic and interesting at home; and stopping being such a slob. Even larger changes of lifestyle are possible. There are plenty of avenues.

For men who lack inner security, however, the loss of sexual contact is devastating – far beyond its actual meaning. The average man – shut down to his feelings since childhood, numb and tense in his body – only really feels alive when he is having sex. Sex is the only opening to his inner world. Now this avenue is lost, too.

The problem may go deeper still. Lacking adequate fathering, he has never really unbonded from his mother. He has simply transferred his mother-needs on to his wife. So, as well as a loss of sex, he experiences a loss of love at an infantile level. It's as if he's been left in his crib to starve. Many men in their late thirties and early forties have encountered this despair. The drowned school-teacher at the start of this book was an instance of this. The depression that arises is so complete that all previous enjoyments and reasons for living seem to have turned to ashes.

The man in this position usually acts in a weak and helpless way. This just makes him even less appealing to his wife, however much she may sympathise. (She would do him no favour by relenting.) Or he may get nasty, become violent, start a secret bank account, visit prostitutes or begin having an affair. This is almost always a serious mistake. With the new woman, he will simply replay the pattern. (Five years down the track, he will be at the same place. He finds himself, at 45, walking the boards with another sleepless baby, thinking, 'I've been here before'.)

Listen carefully here. It isn't a woman you need at this time in your life. This whole catastrophe of the long dark night of the penis is the result of a totally mistaken belief on the part of the man that you can't live without a woman's love. The remedy – vitally important since we are talking about half of all British marriages here – is for other men to step in and give emotional support.

This is not the same as getting you drunk. Good friends at these times will listen to you talk about your problems but also have fun, take you fishing, eat, cook and play. They will also, when the time is right, point out that it's time you got back to your family and sorted things out.

It's as if male friends and elders bathe your wounds, remind you that life is good, give you a hug and then throw you back into the ring.

Choose your friends carefully. Some friends are on the side of your marriage and your happiness. However, other men are losers with women and are glad to see you having problems too. They don't want you to stay married. Women-fearing men can be found in every bar in every city of the world. They'd love your company.

The man who has made it through

For the man who makes it through the long dark night, the rewards are great. He loses the baby-like quality of most men, and becomes more straight-backed and fierce-eyed. He is no longer in any hurry. He is very different around women – more companionable, humorous, direct. He is no longer 'mother-bound' or sleazy. Comfortable in his aloneness, he approaches women as equals. Since he offers a woman real friendship and not a big empty barrel for them to fill, he is much more attractive. There's sweet irony here that when you can 'take it or leave it', when love and affection are no longer a matter of life and death, then it all comes to you.

There will always be tension in male–female relationships: adult love isn't meant to have the same sugary-sweet harmony of a mother and baby. When an adult man and woman meet, expect sparks. Learning to dance with this tension, to use it and enjoy it as a way of defining and refining your own identity, sharing in the making of a home, raising kids, finding your place in the community and world, men and women can give each other enormous joy, and only a dash or two of grief for flavour.

In a nutshell

♦ Don't agree with your wife for the sake of peace. Say what is true for you. You have to walk a line – not giving in out of weakness and not bullying either. Both are signs of unnecessary fear.

♦ Men are less skilled in verbal debate, having been given less training as boys. But you are the expert on you. Hang in there, keep talking, till you get the knack.

♦ Decide now never to use violence against a woman or child. If you have trouble with this, join a men's programme that addresses this problem.

♦ In sex and loving, the man has to make the running much of the time. This is a matter of biology. Learn to be persistent and courtly. Be protective. Don't crowd her. Work to win her over. If sometimes you don't succeed, don't take it personally.

♦ Most marriages go through phases of sexual distance or shutting down. Don't mistake this for not being lovable. At the same time, don't depress yourself and tolerate an unhappy sex life. Work to find out what is wrong, and fix it. Make sure your life is balanced with male company, and that you have satisfying and creative outlets other than being with your partner. Love returns more quickly if you don't need it. Your partner is not your mother.

Other voices

··

Something awful happens to many men after they get married. As a sensitive and aware married woman I interviewed described the married men in her neighbourhood: 'They're all so passive. They have to hate their wives because those guys are hardly even people. A typical weekend day for them seems to mean trimming hedges, mowing the lawns and puttering with their cars.' Furthermore, many married men seem to become progressively more childlike, dependent and helpless in their interactions with their wives. Wives discussing their husbands with me in private often make comments such as, 'He acts like a baby', 'He's become so dependent on me it scares me. He won't do anything for himself', 'He acts as if he's totally helpless', and 'He's always hanging around the house and getting in the way. I wish he had some more friends.'

Many of these men ask their wives for permission whenever they want to do things on their own. When they describe the positive aspects of their marriage relationship it often sounds something like, 'She lets me do a lot of things on my own and doesn't stay on my back, like a lot of other wives that I know.' In essence, the wife has been given the role of permission-giver or mother-figure by the male.

Progressively, the married man begins to distrust his own judgement and taste. He starts to believe that he is an unaesthetic clod who is only good in the business or working world and that his taste does not measure up to hers. Like mother, she knows best. As one real-estate person expressed it to me, 'I never sell to the husband. I always sell to the wife. If he likes the house, it doesn't mean anything. But if she likes it, I've got a sale.'

Because he is caught in a relationship that may not be intrinsically satisfying to him, although he is not always in conscious touch with his anger, resentment and desire for autonomy, his negative feelings continually emerge indirectly in the form of passive aggression. He is 'in' the relationship but not 'of' it. The passive expression of his frustration and discontent assumes many forms:

1. Extreme moodiness and occasional outbursts of rage that are precipitated by relatively minor things, such as a misplaced sock, laundry done late, a button that hasn't been sewn on, a toy left on the floor or a late meal.

2. Grabbing for the mail, a drink, and then hiding behind the newspaper or in front of a television set almost immediately after coming home from work.

3. Increasing expression of his wanting to be 'left alone' when he's at home.

4. Increasing complaints of fatigue and physical ailments, such as backaches, stomach-aches and headaches.

5. A drifting of attention when his wife is speaking to him, causing him to ask her frequently to repeat herself, an indication that his mind is wandering and that he is not concentrating.

6. Having to be reminded constantly about the same things which he continually seems to forget, such as hanging up his clothes, taking out the garbage, etc.

7. A general resistance to talking about his day when he comes home in the evening.

8. Avoidance of sexual intimacy manifested indirectly by either coming to bed after she's fallen asleep, or falling asleep before she's come to bed. Other manifestations include bringing home work from the office and doing it into the

night, and staying up late to read or watch television.

9. An avoidance of eye contact with his wife.

10. An increasing tendency to confine his social life with his wife to activities such as going out to eat or to a movie, which do not require active interaction between them.

11. Generalised feelings of boredom. The boredom often disguises an impulse or desire to do things or be places other than where he is. Since he is unable to own up to his real needs, he does nothing and sits home bored instead.

Unable to assert himself openly or to own up to his discomfort, his hidden resentment emerges in myriad underground ways. The message he is transmitting indirectly to his wife is, 'I'm afraid to do what I really want to do, or express how I really feel, so I'll avoid feeling guilty by staying at home. But you aren't going to get any satisfaction from my presence either.'

Herb Goldberg, *The New Male*

Does it hold true today in your opinion?

Chapter 7

Being a Real Father

What does fathering mean? Listen to the language we use every day and it will tell you a lot. If we talk of 'mothering' children, we get a picture of caring, nurturing and spending long hours in close, sensitive contact. The word 'fathering' means something quite different. You can father a child in two minutes (in the back seat of a car), which makes you nothing more than a source of sperm. Many people today see no problem with single women or lesbian couples seeking donor insemination, leaving fathers – as people – completely out of the equation. However, fathering is much more than this. It's an essential part of raising children of either sex. Yet the art of fatherhood has almost been lost from our homes and communities.

John Embling is a worker with inner-city kids in Australia, helping to pull them back from homelessness, violence and imprisonment. Here, from his book

Fragmented Lives, are his thoughts on fathers:

> I spend most of my life with children, young adults, mothers, but where are the fathers? [Over 10 years] I have known only four or five fathers-as-parents, as providers, as role models…I have seen so many young children who need men in their home lives, men who are capable of psychologically meeting their needs.
>
> Even the strongest, most capable single parent finds it difficult to give his or her child all that is needed to make a human being. But what about the single, deserted, penniless mother on [a deprived housing estate]. Where do her children look for relationships with father figures?
>
> I often look around for the fathers in the lives of our children. I feel a sense of profound loss, of defeat, of inhumanity, as I see men devoid of personal contact with their children. Their loss, the loss of something central to the human process, is also our loss. Something is being crippled, and all the money, technology, bureaucracy, professionalism, ideology in the world won't make it right again.

The role of father has sunk to a very low point. Are fathers necessary? One feminist writer once said, 'A world without men would be a world full of fat, happy women.' To which we'd add, '…and very screwed-up children'.

This chapter argues that both boys and girls need fathers for specific reasons in their development – reasons that cannot be fulfilled by mothers on their own. Even more importantly, we believe that boys who do not get active fathering either by their own father or someone willing to step in will never get their lives as men to work. It's as simple and as absolute as that.

Let's assume you are a father or plan to be one. You have love and good intentions, but still you may be operating in a virtual vacuum. Many of the elements you wish to bring to parenting your children – consistency, firmness, warmth and involvement – you may have never received from a male figure yourself. You want to pass on the river of healthy masculinity to your children, even though you have received only a trickle yourself. Or, to use a more modern metaphor, the software has been lost. There is a problem in turning your love into action.

Fathering involves a great deal more than providing sperm.

Fathers today are highly motivated, even desperate, to get it right, often because they feel so acutely that their own childhoods were inadequate and painful. Many men's groups spend much of their time sharing ideas and helping each other to be better dads. Groups around the world have also been started by support agencies, such as Barnados, Parents Advice Centres, the YMCA (with its excellent dads-and-lads and dads-and-daughters programmes), to help each other with their children (uncling, if you like). They may organise Saturday events, day trips, camping expeditions and so forth, creating more opportunities for their children to be with their own fathers, and also get to know other good men and experience the variety and richness of men of different ages in a safe and positive environment. What we once had as our birthright in our villages a hundred or even ten thousand years ago is being recreated, and the results are very good.

Dropping the old roles

Much parenting is done unconsciously. We find ourself saying and doing the things our parents did, and if those were bad, then we are in trouble. The first step to being a good dad is to shed some of the old and toxic role models. These were often limiting and impoverished, and yet sit heavily like old videotape collections in our head. Unless we get rid of these tapes, all it takes is someone to accidentally hit the play button and we will activate them all over again – speaking and behaving to our children the way our fathers spoke and acted towards us.

Author John Lee, in *At My Father's Wedding*, describes four kinds of defective father that existed in the past. Here they are, loosely paraphrased.

The man who would be king

This was the man who, having (presumably) worked hard all day, returned home to be waited on by his loyal wife-servant and seen-but-not-heard children. He was king of the house and ruled his castle kingdom from his armchair. His family tiptoed around him, careful not to 'bother' him. The only time this father got really involved was to dish out punishments or pardons. This was also the wait-until-your-father-gets-home father.

> My dad had an over-developed attachment to his roof. He talked about his roof a lot, and referred to it constantly when I dared question the king's decree for me. 'This is my house. You live under my roof. As long as you are under my roof, you'll do as you're told. When you get your own roof you can do whatever you want to, but while you're under my roof, you'll do what I say when I say it.' 'Damn,' I thought to myself. 'I can't wait to get my own roof.'

The critical father

Full of put-downs and nit-picking, driven by his own frustration and anger, this father was certainly active in the family, but in totally negative, frightening ways. 'Is that the best you can do?' 'Can't you get anything right?' 'You stupid idiot, look what you've done!' Whatever was frustrating him – his job, his own father, his lack of success in life, even his unexpressed love for his children – was turned into an acid that ate away at his children's well-being. Sometimes this kind of father had no idea how he came across. He thought he was just being helpful and involved. But his kids ended up hating him because there was no positivity or gentleness.

The passive father

This guy gave up all duties, responsibilities and power to his wife, the mother. He also backed down to the kids, his boss, relatives, society and the government. Homer Simpson is this kind of dad most of the time. He has no backbone, apart from occasionally losing his temper. For the most part, it's all just too hard even to think about. Apart from an occasional sarcastic comment or half-hearted whinge, he was never really there. Unable to stand the heat, he would retreat into a newspaper, TV, alcohol, his job, or his garden shed. His kids, especially his boys, grew up hating him for what he wasn't.

The absent father

This man might have been a capable, even powerful man, but not in the family arena. He was off having a career, leaving early and returning late at night. When he made love to your mother to start you, he was thinking about something else. He wasn't at your sports events or your school concert. He might have paid for all kinds of goodies for you, and even been quite polite and kindly if you passed him in the hall, but he wasn't any use to you as a father because a father has to be there for hours, not minutes, a day in order to pass on his gifts.

So those are the familiar models, which we can easily recognise in our childhoods, and in ourselves today. But there is a huge and well-documented revolution already happening in Britain today, and in other Western countries. Younger fathers are infinitely more hands-on, enjoy their children and want to know them fully. When I travel I always ask old women at bus stops and railway stations, 'What has changed?' They point to dads pushing prams. That was unheard of in their time. They find it a very welcome change.

The time fathers spend with children has quadrupled in the last two decades, according to some studies, and a rising number of fathers are the primary carer while their partner works, or are the sole parents after divorce. A quarter of single-parent families are headed by dads.

It's not so hard, if you are willing to learn as you go along. Those of us who had good fathers remember all the little things: playing with us when we were small, taking us to school, buying shoes or a jacket, playing in the garden, going to sports days, setting rules, deciding on what happens when those rules are broken, bathing us, tending us when we were sick. We remember the kindness and patience, the givingness of it all, which we simply took for granted, but are now in awe of. Those of us who had few of these things find our way, determined to learn and get it right.

How men and boys were split

For hundreds of thousands of years the human race lived in small nomadic groups of, at most, 30 people. Perhaps in your whole life, if you had lived in those times, you would meet only 200 people. Even when the New Stone Age ended around 4000 BC and recorded history began, we lived only in villages and very small towns until very recent times.

In the timeless rhythm of village and tribal life, men were deeply involved in raising the children. You still see this today in the developing world – men carrying toddlers to the fields on their shoulders, sons and nephews learning from the older men as they go through the day. Along with the skills of hunting and making things, boys were learning how to be a man. It was a long apprentice-ship: 40-year-olds were still learning. Old men and women led the community by virtue of their vast knowl-edge and experience. All day, every day, boys drank in the tone, style and manner of being a man from a dozen or so available role models, who were tough but also tender with them, as needed.

Surprisingly to most of us, it's now thought by anthro-pologists that life in hunter gatherer times was relatively easy, even leisurely. Knowing hundreds of useful plants and the ways of animals meant that food gathering relied on skill more than exertion. The desert Aboriginal people in my part of Australia (a very harsh environment) could meet their food and shelter needs with only a couple of hours' effort per day. (We've clearly gone backwards.) Certainly in our prehistory there was famine, disease and warfare, but these were interruptions in a timeless pattern of relative plenty. This pattern depended on each new generation becoming skilled, safe, integrated members of the community. Nothing consumed as much time and energy as the training and socialisation of the young, so they did it well.

Then, suddenly, in an unprecedented way (in the ecological blink of an eye), it all began to change. Beginning barely 200 years ago, the Industrial Revolution arrived and changed everything. In the British Isles, for instance, villagers were driven from their homes in tens of thousands to free up the land for sheep, as wool production was more profitable than crops and took much less labour. Whole villages were razed by the landlords' hired men, so the inhabitants could never return. Men away in the Napoleonic Wars returned to find their homes gone, their families sometimes starved to death. The Potato Famine in Ireland was the last event of a long genocide against the peasant classes across Britain. The towns needed factory workers, miners and labourers. It was a matter of change or die. (The same pattern is still taking place all across Asia and Africa today.)

In the new industrial era fathers, for the first time in history, worked away from their families, waking before first light and returning after dark, six days a week. When fathers came home they were exhausted, angry and defeated men. The children learnt to avoid them. Mothers struggled to raise the children, school regimes were intended to subdue and condition them. For the first time in human history a generation of boys grew up without being fathered in the true sense. Today we take this arrangement for granted: fathers work, mothers raise children (or put them in daycare for other women to raise). Female schoolteachers civilise our boys. Boys have a choice: to comply and be good or to misbehave. The 'misbehavers' form gangs for solace and self-protection, looking for the masculine energy they do not realise they are missing.

> **When asked about the father doll, they replied, 'He's at work.'**

Father-absence today

From a son's point of view, little has changed for 150 years. Now fathers work in cleaner, safer environments, but the effect on the family is the same. It could even be worse. A man who takes up desk work in an office has little in common with his son and often cannot even explain to him what he is doing. Daddy 'goes to work', where he simply disappears into incomprehensible activity for nine or 10 hours a day.

In the mid-1970s the Mattel toy company wanted to market a family of dolls called the Heart Family. First they field-tested the sets, which comprised (naturally) a mother, father and two children. The test children, in numerous trials, took the father doll and set him aside. Then they played with the mother and children. When asked, 'What about the father doll?' they replied, 'He's at work.' Father's work had no substance or meaning to these children, and he was rarely used in the make-believe play. (Eventually, of course, the problem was solved. The father dolls were sold separately with big muscles, armour and a gun.)

When a father is around for only an hour or two at night, the mother's values and style become the values and style of the house. Dad is a kind of visitor, a shadowy figure. Something is missing. For boys there is no experience of maleness in action. What children get from a career father is not his energy, or his teaching, or his substance, but only his mood. And at seven o'clock at night, that mood is mostly irritation and fatigue.

For girls it's different – they can learn to be a woman from Mum and her friends, but the boys cannot learn to be a man. Immersed in the talk of women, a girl would grow into an articulate and self-aware woman. The boy would have to make up his masculinity from imagination, the movies and his friends.

A spectrum of experiences characterised twentieth-century families. Some men managed in spite of everything to be a strong and loving presence in their family. One man told me, 'Dad was away all week, he was a biscuit salesman. But on Saturdays he would tell Mum to stay in bed or go out with her friends, and he would cook for us, play with us, take us swimming in the summer. Saturdays were Dad days, and they were heaven.' On the other extreme, almost half of marriages collapsed under the strain, and many children grew up with no man at all in the home. (One study found that a year after a divorce, a third of men no longer saw their children at all.)

The gang as a substitute dad

In communities where fathers are mostly absent, whether affluent or poor, the phenomenon of the teenage gang can be found. As mid-adolescence arrives, boys hunger for some outward movement into the world of men. In fact, this need is so strong that they will follow anyone: even a 17-year-old can be perceived as a father substitute by a lonely boy of 14. Yet the 17-year-old has little wisdom to impart, and is not in charge of his own impulses, let alone those of others. Disaster stalks close at hand. Teenage gangs do not occur in communities where the different ages interact and care for each other – they are a symptom of a community in trouble. The gang members' behaviour (which they themselves do not consciously understand) is clearly designed to provoke older adult males into taking notice of them. Small-town policemen who know their jobs are fully aware of this; they are acting as the community's surrogate dad, and it's the kids without dads that give them all their challenges.

Parents worry about peer group pressure leading their child into drugs, sex or crime. They should take note that the greatest predictor of peer group problems is a poor relationship with the same-sex parent. (For girls it's the mother–daughter relationship, for boys the father–son.) A teenage boy who enjoys the company and involvement of his father and his father's friends does not need to look towards a 17-year-old gang leader for leadership. These boys will be still be part of a peer group, but they have the inner strength to hold back from any stupidities the group may wander into and, in fact, will exercise leadership naturally as a result of their healthy linkage back to more mature maleness.

Confident maleness

Even in intact families, where fathers care and want to do their best, the demands of the workplace mitigate against success. It's highly likely that boys have a biological need for several hours of one-to-one male contact per day. To have a demanding job, commute to work in a city and raise sons well is extremely hard. Something has to give.

It gets worse still. A number of psychoanalysts and family therapists around the world have noted that father-absence creates some special side-effects. It isn't just that the absent father is a neutral persona. You can't be neutral in a family – occupants of the same household can only love or hate each other. A son either loves or hates his father – it's rarely an indifferent relationship. Having something you deeply need so near and yet so far produces a great intensity of feeling.

The modern career dad has these problems to contend with. Men in the past showed their love by working hard and long: the father as a walking wallet. But, sadly, we do not get appreciated for it since it is our presence, not our bounty, that is hungered for by our children. (Of course, they want our bounty too. But kids will be happy with less if they have Dad's time and attention.)

Women need to be very clear about what they ask of their husbands since men are likely, by default, to assume that it is their earning capacity that is their biggest contribution. A friend of ours, a bank manager, married a very beautiful woman who once mentioned during their courtship that she would never have married a 'loser'. He became a compulsive gambler to keep up the impression of success. This led to him embezzling several million dollars from his bank – and going to prison for several years. His wife left him for another man. It was a tough lesson.

Men have to talk to their children. The twentieth-century father was strong and silent. But what use is that to a growing boy? He needs to know the words, the feelings, the values. He needs a man who will share enough of his inner world for him to begin to form his own. And he needs to see a man acting from his values – to learn how relationships work. One man told me, 'My parents never argued or fought in front of us kids. They went into the bedroom, and you couldn't hear what was being said. When it came to fighting in my own marriage, I didn't know how to do it. My wife wondered why I was asking her to come to the bedroom.'

It takes a lot of verbal skill to navigate life and relationships at work and at home. All through the twentieth century, girls received this skill – they grew up with women around them all day, every day. They soaked in the example of many competent, varied and expressive women. By the time they were adults, their femaleness was like a broad, strong pyramid to stand on. Boys, however, received so little male contact that their masculinity was like perching on a wavery stack of empty cans. How could they feel anything other than insecure? In arguments, in discussions at work or home they were lost. 'She puts her case so well. Her words are so well chosen. Even when she is wrong, she sounds right. All her friends agree.' But how can he articulate himself? What has he to draw on? Faced with this, a man may cave in or run away, or, worst of all, hit out. In counselling I often encounter men who simply cannot be honest with their partners. Couple counselling is almost useless in this situation. The men first need help to find their own voice and develop their sense of self. It's not that they lie, but that they cannot find the truth – their truth. It leads to enormous grief. Without confidence to put your case, nothing can be resolved. And confidence, for a man, depends on extensive contact with healthy and diverse kinds of older men.

Getting it right

What can a man do? For a start, show up in your own children's lives. Begin during pregnancy: if your unborn baby hears your voice often, it will turn to face you once it is born, recognising that familiar rumble.

When your baby is small, hold it against you often and it will feel as well as hear your voice. A man's voice resonates deep in his chest and vibrates through a held baby in a way it will come to love.

When you take the baby into your arms at the moment of birth, have your shirt open. Do not use soap, deodorant or scented cosmetics of any kind. Let your child bond to the natural, clean, sweaty smell of you. Your unique odour will become reassuring to the baby. Don't be separated from your wife and child in the hospital. Sleep in the room, care for the child so that your wife can get some sleep. Of course, respect her wish to have time alone with the child, too. Do not let the nurses take your child off to a nursery when it can have its own parents' care. Organise some time off work for at least a month, or three months if you can, so that the early days can be unhurried. Teach yourself to cook.

Watch for competitive feelings. On the cover of *Families and How to Survive Them* by John Cleese and Robin Skynner there is a cartoon of a man watching his wife breast-feed the new baby. The man is sucking a dummy and looking very unhappy. When a new baby arrives, watch out for and acknowledge competitive feelings arising in you. Your wife loves you as well as the baby, but in the first year it's natural for her to switch hormonally to the kind of devotion that makes her able to care for the child and love doing it. Support her, find a few minutes a day with her just to link up, and be patient. She needs you and she will come back to you.

Being there for your son

The Cleese–Skynner book also includes a simple and profound cartoon in which a boy walks across a bridge over a river, from his mother's side to his father's. The mother looks worried, the father smiles shyly. This symbolises an essential stage in male development. Around the age of six the primary identification of the boy seems to switch. He will still love and relate intensely to his mother, but he is not hers quite so much any more. He actively wants to be with and be like his father. It's not that he is leaving the mother, so much as adding the father to the picture. The boy can do this only if his father is around, available and interested in sharing time with him – doing things with him, good-naturedly challenging and testing him, but never wounding or belittling him. Here are some ways to do this.

Play-wrestling

If you want to get along well with boys, you have to learn to wrestle. Children of both sexes love to get down on the floor and play rough and tumble, be held in the air, be tickled, try to pin your arms down, play games of all kinds. Boys who feel secure love their fathers or other men to do this with them; they are excited by the competition of matching strength and agility, and love the closeness as well.

Several important and symbolic lessons are being learnt while doing this seemingly fun activity. The first is 'not hurting'. Inevitably, a child wrestling on the carpet will hurt an adult by being too boisterous, not careful enough with an elbow or a knee. If this happens, the father stops the action and says clearly to the boy, 'Your body is precious. My body is precious. So we need one or two rules, like not kneeing or hitting. Can you handle that?'

The boy usually agrees. It will happen more than once, of course, and be handled the same way. The aim is to learn how to fight without harm, to use lots of strength but not hurt themselves or others. A potent lesson is being learnt here. When the boy is older, he will almost always be stronger and larger than his girlfriend or wife. He must know how to debate, take criticism, experience strong emotions and, at the same time, never use his physical strength to dominate or hurt her. The restraint learnt from actual wrestling will come in handy in the verbal wrestling all couples need to do from time to time. The boy learns to contain his strength from the example of a father who never hurts him and who doesn't allow him to hurt others.

Winding up and winding down

There is a unique pattern of play that fathers all over the world seem to demonstrate. I'm grateful to Alastair Spate, for the following well-written account:

> Imagine two parents on a living-room floor with a two-year-old-boy and a pile of blocks. The mother encourages the child to play with the blocks and at least construct a pile or some sort of rough structure. Typically, at some stage, the father will transform himself into a roaring monster-cum-bulldozer, knock over the bricks and provoke peals of delight in the child. From then, the two males 'wind up' in challenge and response, giggling and hooting, rivalling each other to make the biggest mess.
>
> When the father eventually senses some disapproval, or at least concern, in the mother, he begins to 'wind down' the play until a

breathless equilibrium returns to the room and the boy rests in the arms of either of the parents.

This sort of play is very much the father's speciality. The crucial thing is the winding down. Here a father teaches his child, through play, the mastery of his energy and angers, sets the limits of aggression and how to stay in charge of one's emotions and not be flooded by them.

Most readers will have seen the uncontrolled inner and outer rages and depressions of the under-fathered boy, whose first experience of male limit-setting is likely to be the police, truant officer or warden in early adolescence – and by then he is literally a marked man. (Or marked and not yet a man.) He never learnt through this uniquely fatherly play how to become the master in his own house of angers, dreams, yearnings and energy.

And you thought you were just playing! 'Winding oneself down' turns out to be a vital, life-saving skill learnt on the living-room floor or the back lawn. It frees you from being overtaken by your own emotions. This is the gift a good, physically comfortable father can give.

Identifying an under-fathered boy

Boys who are under-fathered can be diagnosed easily. They fall into two distinct types. One type takes on macho mania: the wearing of 'aggressive' clothes, collecting violent toys and comics, or (if older) carrying knives and obsessively studying weapons and war. This type of boy will usually be quickly drawn into dubious friendships with other neglected boys or young men. At least these gangs provide some sense of belonging and self-esteem, as well as a measure of physical protection.

The other type is under-confident, a mummy's boy, is often very depressed and frequently a school refuser. Younger boys of this type may also have problems with bedwetting or soiling. They tend to get picked on at school, are reluctant to try new things or go to new places, and often have irrational fears of illness or accident.

Both these types suffer from the same problem: father hunger. Mothers will often not be able to fix this problem on their own. As a father, it's your job, and time, activity, warmth and involvement are your tools.

Discipline

In the bad old days, fathers were the disciplinarian, the enforcer. The fact that they were away from the house all day made them more scary. 'Wait till your father gets home!' was the last-ditch threat of exhausted and desperate mums. Today the scene is quite different. Wimpish fathers are everywhere. They leave discipline to their wives or, worse still, undermine them: 'Let the kids be – they aren't being that bad. Just relax, dear, it doesn't really matter.' (Such men are in for a short marriage and a terrible sex life.)

Women and children need men to be at least equal partners in discipline. A man who can add his weight through clear and direct talk, without the need for a big confrontation, is a huge benefit to a family. There is also another reason why fathers need to take a tougher role. The feelings of a mother for her child are primarily tender, and the child reciprocates this. If a great deal of disciplining is being done by the mother, especially if it is negative and critical, a boy can start to feel that his mother hates him. Many mothers tell me, 'Every time I open my mouth, it's to criticise.' A boy can feel the mother love eroding. If the father is playing his part, though, the mother relaxes, feels supported and is less likely to get tired and negative.

If a boy sees Mum and Dad working together in discipline, backing each other up, he calms down more easily.

Discipline only really works when parent and child already have a loving connection established – a trust fund of good experiences together. That's why the disciplinarian dad of old was so hated. He didn't do enough good things with you, so it was easy to believe he was doing discipline because he hated you.

The essence of good discipline is to get engaged, eyeball to eyeball, and be definite so that children can state their case but are also made to listen to yours. This is quite the opposite of the techniques of isolation, star charts and mechanical means that modern psychology often recommends in the home or school. Children today do not need more remoteness. They need you to get involved.

Mother–son conflict

As Douglas Gillette explained in *Wingspan*, an anthology of writings about the men's movement:

> One of the most important developmental tasks, which a boy must successfully accomplish in order to achieve satisfying intimate relationships with women later in life, is that of separating emotionally from the mother. The boy must come to experience himself as profoundly independent of his mother – of her emotional states, of her needs and of her sexual identity.

In his mid-teens, a boy needs to be able to recognise that he can live without his mother. The better the job she has done in nurturing and teaching him, the more vital it is that he realises he can stand alone and not need her. If he's to make space in his heart to live independently, to get close to other women of his own age, he needs to move away just a little from his mother. If this stage goes well, he will return to her as a friend, with lifelong depth and warmth. If it does not, which in modern men is often the case, their relationship will be awkward, and he may remain strangely and compulsively juvenile and impotent around her, and around other women, sometimes for the rest of his life.

The father, and other men who can and should be part of the boy's world, provide a safe anchor so that the son can distance from his mother, and yet still find the world a supportive place. The boy moves progressively out into the larger world by widening his circles of support.

Some of this seems to be 'wired in' and explains much typical and rather disruptive behaviour. Around the age of 14 (when hormone levels surge and testosterone rises to about eight times its base level) boys will intuitively begin to distance from mothers. Without knowing why, they will pick fights, act disrespectfully, argue and generally make themselves unattractive. A caveman type of scene often occurs, where the boy may be rude or aggressive to his mother over some small matter. The father, hearing this going on, will stride in and use those time-honoured words, 'Don't speak to your mother like that'. The message is twofold: to the woman that she has an ally and need never feel intimidated in her own home; to the boy that these adults are aligned as a team and committed to him growing up well.

This isn't to imply that his wife can't take care of herself, only that she doesn't have to do it alone. This scene, which many of us remember, is a sign that everything is on track. A lone mother must manage this time with great care because, without any help, it can so easily slide into yelling or hitting, an impossible situation for mother and son. She must deflect things by saying something like this: 'We're both too emotional right now. Let's leave it for a couple of hours and talk about it when we've cooled down.' Later she can talk with her son about the need for them both to get along and have some basic rules of respect. (In extreme cases, she may have to make this a rule of the boy being able to stay living in the home, but it's better if both parties can agree as equals that they won't be disrespectful.) A single mother will need a great deal of humour and support from friends at this stage. A grandfather, uncle or man friend who can talk with the boy at this age, pointing out the need for respecting his mother, is very helpful.

A son thus makes a three-step journey: he bonds with his mother as a new baby; he adds Dad into the equation, especially into his mid-teens; and then there comes a time when a father is not enough either.

A mentor for your son

Even the best of fathers cannot raise their sons alone. Fathers need extra help from other men to do this properly. In tribal situations the whole male community got involved with the teenage boys, mentoring, training and initiating them. A father never had to do this alone; he could count on all kinds of help, and boys could count on positive input usually more relaxed and accepting than fathers manage to be.

A boy in his mid- to late teens needs other men to step in, who will teach him skills, give him a sense of worth and take him out beyond the family walls. In other words, he needs a mentor or two. His own father may be a mentor to someone else's son. Different from fathering, mentoring is an informing but less emotionally charged role. In the old days the mentor, not the father, was the person who taught a boy his craft for life. This arrangement took the heat out of the father–son relationship, which can get very tense, as anyone who has taught their teenager to drive a car knows only too well.

> *A fishing club isn't really about fishing, or a football club about football.*

In practice, this means a few simple steps. If you have sons, you also need to have groups of male friends whom they can be around, so that they feel accepted into the adult male world. While a father and son will, with luck, share some interests, the mentors may widen the range and prevent the son being limited to what the father can offer. There will always be deeply intellectual fathers with athletic and extrovert sons, and vice versa. This needn't be a problem if the father is willing to allow and encourage good men from among his acquaintances to supplement what he offers and so create a balanced adolescent experience. As John Palmour observes in *Wingspan*:

> A boy needs help to learn about his own gifts and identity, and help to learn how to identify someone who has mastered the skills that are the birthright of his nature. Their lives seldom expose them to mature men doing things of such quality as to inspire a boy's emulation and his willingness to discipline himself in anticipation of being ready for his own chance later in life. In this light, we should not be surprised that our teenagers have grown apathetic about preparing for roles that are either invisible to them or that exercise no charm over their imaginations.

Wise parents understand that the myriad activity groups around which people organise their leisure time serve a more important purpose. A fishing club isn't really about fishing, or a football league about football (though part of the activity involves treating these things as being of extraordinary importance). They are really just ways that men can care for each other and take boys into tutelage, give them positive messages and thus provide a vehicle for character growth and development. Today this is often misunderstood and the point of the activity is lost, such as when competition becomes too intense, or coaches encourage cheating or violence on the field, or the use of steroids. Done well, though, these activities give our sons a tribe to belong to. They can inspire and help him to find his true direction and philosophy for life.

What a single mother can do

Single mothers I speak with are usually very alert to the need for male role models for their sons. Once they find a way to meet this need, many problems of young sons, such as shyness or aggressiveness, are much reduced. If you are a single mother of a boy in primary school, ask the school if he can be in a class with a good male teacher at least once or twice during his time there. Get your son to choose those athletic, musical or scouting options that have good men in them. Be choosy and ask yourself: are these the kind of men I want my son to turn into? Be careful: sometimes sexually abusive men prey on fatherless boys, exploiting their hunger for male affection, but don't keep them away from all men for fear of this taking place.

Men are most helpful when they are clear on what their job is. A mother in a ToughLove group (a self-help group for parents of kids in trouble) told how her 14-year-old son simply would not get out of bed and go to school in the mornings. Several men from her group offered to go, as a team, and rouse her son from bed to get him off to school. They showed up in the boy's room one morning and urged him firmly but good-naturedly through the morning routine. The boy was shocked and somewhat amazed that anyone cared. After a couple of visits, they had only to drop in briefly, then be on call. The boy got his act together.

Single mothers can raise boys well, but not alone. They need the help of a network of friends and family. They have to take care of themselves to avoid building up negativity or flying off the handle, and maintain good humour, especially around the mid-teens. It takes a village to raise a child, and the village needs to have both women and men.

Fathers with daughters

Daughters need some special things from fathers. One of these is affirmation. This means the feeling of being appreciated, admired but never invaded or exploited, so that they can practise conversation and mutual admiration with a 'safe' male. Through talking with their fathers and other older men, daughters can gain assurance, feel worthwhile and know they do not need the first boy who looks at them. Knowing how to be comfortable around men is priceless for a girl.

The quality of her mother's and father's relationship is important too. Knowing that her father aligns with her mother at a deep level and can't be seduced or undermined means that she recognises boundaries. She learns how to say no and take no for an answer. If Mum and Dad get along well, she will want at least that quality of relationship in her own marriage.

Fathers of teenage daughters will naturally feel some caution and suspicion towards boyfriends. Within reason, this is useful. It doesn't hurt for boyfriends to be moderately terrified. But don't be so scary that your daughter can't bring them home; it's better to know and meet them. Some clear safety limits can be set, appropriate for the daughter's age and stage. A social worker friend of mine, who is divorced from his first wife, learnt that his 13-year-old daughter was at a party with some people who were far beyond her ability to deal with. He quickly telephoned two large male friends of his, and together they went and got her. She made a token complaint, but was basically very relieved.

Being trustworthy is something a teenager has to prove, it isn't a right. At the same time, a father has to guard against being jealous out of his own needs. He has to envisage his daughter moving out, being strong in making her own choices, having a happy life. No one will ever be good enough for her, but luckily it isn't his choice.

Fathers are the first man in a girl's life. It is now believed by researchers into family dynamics that this sets her expectations about all men, and strongly affects her choice of mate. If her father is abusive, she may find herself attracted to abusive men. If he is distant, she will choose distant men. If her father is kind, treats her with respect, is interested in her and her views, she will choose a mate with these qualities. Such is the awesome power – to bless or to wound – that fathers carry.

Defending and protecting

To a boy a father should represent strength and protection. For some little boys this can be life-changing. One client of mine, Sean, was sent to boarding school at the age of nine. He had been there for only two weeks when the head teacher called him into his office, locked the door and began to sexually abuse him. The head gave dire threats to the boy should he ever tell anyone. The abuse was repeated many times during that first term.

When Sean's father visited the school at the end of term, the principal met with him to discuss Sean's progress. Sean was summoned to the office and immediately took in the scene. The powerful monster-teacher, smug at his desk; his father, without a chair to sit on, perched on a wooden firebox beside the hearth. Instinctively, Sean knew that his father had no power or confidence in this place. He said nothing about the sexual abuse to his father, who left, oblivious. Sean remembers to this day the smile the head gave him as his father departed. The abuse continued all that year.

Young men need protection. Robert Bly speaks angrily about the abuse of young men by the generals in Vietnam. These 19- and 20-year-olds, often with idealistic or religious backgrounds, found themselves immersed in the bloodshed, horror and ethical disaster of Vietnam. Their father-figure generals and lieutenants then sent them to the brothels of Thailand to let off steam, destroying their respect for womanhood or tenderness and completing their disillusionment with life. Tens of thousands of these men committed suicide or retreated into drugs during or since that conflict.

At any age men, through their isolation, can be extraordinarily vulnerable. Several years ago a nurse friend of mine came across an old man crying in the stairwell of a hospital. She asked him what was wrong and he told her that he was to have his tongue surgically cut out that day because it was cancerous. They talked for a while, and by the end of the conversation he had decided to cancel the surgery. He was 84 and wished to live out his life with his ability to speak and taste intact. He might die sooner, but he would die a complete human being.

Shielding young men from soul assaults

There are many assaults on the souls of men, and they begin early. Some women hate all men and will see in male children an avenue of revenge. The son of a friend of mine went for his first day at school. He was a talkative, sparrow-like little boy, full of life. The young female teacher became angry at his chattiness half an hour into the first school lesson of his life. She told him to stand by the waste-paper basket in the corner. He didn't hear her correctly; he thought she said *in* the waste-paper basket, so that is where he stood. She let him stay there for 10 minutes, occasionally ridiculing him to the class.

Unless boys are protected, how else can they keep their tender feelings intact? Unless we bring a nurturing fierce-ness to our lives, how can we ever heal? US author Michael Meade specialises in programmes bringing together men from different races, often in tense ghetto situations. He regularly reads pieces of poetry at these gatherings. As he reads, men begin quietly weeping. Colin Fowler and the Men's Project in Northern Ireland do wonderful healing work in men's retreats, and psycholo-gist Guy Corneau has begun over 600 men's groups across Canada. I have seen the same powerful emotions in men's meetings and forums all over the world. It's clear that enormous amounts of emotional baggage have been carried by boys and men, which has rarely found an outlet other than violence. Not for centuries have men been able to be so open. Something very good and important is beginning to happen.

Protecting your son's sexual development

If you have teenage sons, it's a good idea to let them close their bedroom doors and have some privacy. Don't ever barge in unannounced. Then they can relax about exper-imenting with their bodies. A sensuous and accepting attitude to masturbation is needed in order for boys to learn to be relaxed lovers. The chance to read and see quality erotica – material that shows men and women in equal and enjoyable contact – will help. Never force, invade or push sexuality on to children. Simply allow their natural interest and sense of privacy to be there. Boys will probably obtain soft porn magazines, but these are not appropriate before the age of about 16, and the images shouldn't be plastered on walls. Much of this material is sexist, phony and deceptive in its role-modelling. If accessed too young, boys can get fixated and not move comfortably to relating to real girls. Much material on the Internet is ugly, exploitative and disheartening, and children under 16 should not have computers in their rooms where you cannot see what they are viewing. Let your sons know it's OK to admire women's bodies but always to see women as people A middle path can be found that affirms sexuality, but keeps some specialness around it too.

Avoiding cheapness

In the movie *The Rose*, loosely based on Janis Joplin's life, the heroine (played by Bette Midler) is a blowsy, drug-addicted, past-her-prime rock singer. In one critical scene she is waiting in a recording studio along with some country musicians. She bats her eyes at a young boy in a western shirt, who looks about 17, and he responds, albeit awkwardly. She is about to move into major seduction mode when the boy's father walks into the room, sees what is happening and stops her dead. 'Don't try that cheap slut behaviour with my son,' he tells her.

It's a jolting moment in the film, as we feel her humiliation, but it also feels right. That father is acting admirably. He is a musician too, but out of a different mould, a craftsman, clean-cut and straight-backed, and he is willing to be proactive about right and wrong. What she was doing was, on one level, harmless, even flattering to the young man. On another level it was inappropriate, uncaring, a female form of sexual harassment.

Boys need to understand that girls are capable of misusing them, that a penis can be a handle to get dragged around by. A female office worker in her late teens, interviewed for Bettina Arndt's courageous documentary *When 'No' Means 'Maybe'*, illustrated this perfectly. She talked gaily about the pleasure of getting her dates sexually overheated, only to turn them down. It was a game played for the power buzz it gave her, and she saw no reason to be ashamed.

Police officers have told me that it is not uncommon for a man to visit a prostitute as a last act before he commits suicide. Or is it that loveless sex has pushed a man over the edge? Sex, love, loneliness and desperation can get terribly confused for men, and it's important to talk to boys about the difference between love and lust, and that you will get hurt you if you can't tell the difference.

What if your son is gay?

For some parents, the normal concerns about sexuality are complicated by the discovery that their son is gay. Having a homosexual son or daughter can cause pain because it destroys some of the future aspirations we all hold for our children. The question 'Why?' is often a source of torment, but is really needless. The research on sexual preferences leans heavily towards the die being cast while a baby is still in the womb, and that certain hormonal switching in the brain at this time leads to a young person being gay or lesbian. Still, family dynamics may sometimes play a role. A distant father can set up the conditions for a young man to seek older men in a way that confuses affection and sexuality. Gay clients of mine have often referred to seeking in their lover the father who never loved them. As in a straight relationship, this is bound to cause some grief.

When it's all boiled down, the concerns of parents of gay teenagers are just the same as the concerns of any parent. They want their son to have a happy life. They hope that he will handle his sexuality in a responsible and self-respecting way. And they hope he will find a stable and loving partnership if this is his wish.

Sex, whatever form it takes, is still basically a beautiful and joyful thing. Young gay people discovering their sexuality need acceptance and understanding. They also need a wider society that is not homophobic or persecutory, where healthy role models of gay people are out in the open making good lives for themselves. It's tough enough being a teenager without being in a persecuted minority.

Affirming the sacredness of sex

The urge to conceal details of human sexuality from children is not based just on prudishness. Perhaps it comes from a more ancient understanding that the power of sex is not to be trivialised by passing into minds not yet able to comprehend it.

Sometimes a progressive Christian-, Buddhist- or Islamic-based sex education succeeds far better than the secular forms, which aim to be value-free but just end up sounding mechanical. Religious views at least emphasise the joy of sex and some kind of sacred context in which it takes place. Like putting a wall round a garden, separating it from the mundane increases its beauty.

Part of the problem with sexuality emerging too early is that it prevents the other things that should happen in adolescence. There are other experiences that should come first, such as learning how to be good friends, how to respect other people, how to consider consequences. (David Guterson's book *Snow Falling on Cedars*, and the film based on it, portrays very sensitively how disastrous a sexual relationship could be if it happens at too young an age.)

The teenage years are for forming a clear sense of self. A sexual relationship, with its intensity of emotional as well as physical heat, is challenging at any age. The risk of misjudgement or hurt has to be balanced by a sense of strength. It's the difference between being warmed by the flames, or falling headlong into them. The older one is before entering these relationships, the more likely they are to be navigated happily. But, of course, no one ever waits that long.

Abandoned sons are waiting for their fathers

Many thousands of British boys grow up without knowing their fathers. If you're a separated father, or you were a teen father whose child was adopted, or a father who has been a sperm donor, the thing to remember is that somewhere your son or daughter will be waiting to know you, and to know your side of the story. This won't be from idle curiosity, but because in some deep sense his or her life's progress depends upon it. Whatever you can do to be in contact and give your child access to who and what you are will be of help. Some separated fathers refuse to contact their children, or feel it best not to try. I believe this is a terrible mistake. Even if it's difficult, even if there is hostility and barriers are put in your path, at least find a way to let your child know you think of him, and care, and are ready to know him when he is able to come to you.

Sometimes a teenage son living with his mother will unconsciously start to make life so difficult for her that she will consider letting him go and live with his father. On occasions, to everyone's surprise, this can be just the right thing for finishing off a young man's development. In spite of the difficulties, there is enormous satisfaction and peace of mind if you take on your proper role here. There can be compensations in at least getting parenthood right, if not marriage. Some men have told me they only got close to their children after they were divorced from their wives.

Fatherless children

Are you thinking of divorce? Here is some of what we know about the effect of having a father involved and in the home.

- Boys and girls both have greater self-esteem if their fathers are still in the home. They do better at school, stay at school longer, become better qualified and are more likely to be employed.

- Children with fathers in the home are less likely to be sexually abused, less likely to have trouble with the law and less likely to be beaten up.

- Girls are less likely to be raped or experience premature sexual behaviour or teenage pregnancy.

- Daughters without fathers are more 'malleable' and adapted to pleasing men than are daughters who are secure in a father's love and respect.

- Boys with no fathers, or with fathers who are not around much, are much more likely to be violent, to get into trouble, to do poorly at school and to be a member of a teenage gang in adolescence.

- Families without a man are usually poorer, and children of these families are more likely to move down rather than up the socio-economic ladder.

- Men who are close to their children are less likely to divorce.

- Parents who divorce tend to have kids who divorce too.

The only choice we were given in the past was whether to stay in an unhappy marriage 'for the sake of the kids', or to put our own fulfilment first and leave if a marriage wasn't working. What kids actually need is neither. They need us to be working on our marriage, committed to addressing differences, working at it right there before their eyes.

Assuming it's not a fatally flawed situation of violence, deceit or addiction, we have to make the marriage happier so that we can stay for their sakes and for our own too. I am not saying this is easy, but it is certainly something to be proud of. And even if the marriage is not possible to save, you must still work to be friendly, co-operative and respectful with your ex-partner so that a family can exist even when it's no longer built around a marriage or located in the same home.

In a nutshell

♦ Flush out of your brain the old models:

- The father as an arrogant king

- The father as a judge

- The father as a passive blob

- The father who is hardly ever there

♦ Acknowledge that boys need fathers around many hours a day. Do stuff with your son. The path to closeness with sons is activity together. But be sure to talk too.

♦ Get involved from pregnancy onwards. You can be a presence at every stage in his life, even in the womb.

♦ Wrestle with your children. Teach your boys, through wrestling, to show care and how to be a good loser or winner. Help them to be excited and also teach them when to calm down.

♦ Be a firm but safe disciplinarian. Back up your wife and learn firm love techniques. (My book *More Secrets of Happy Children* focuses on this.)

♦ Be involved with daughters, too. Admire them, teach them self-sufficiency. Respect their space and never evaluate their looks, except positively.

- ◆ Protect your sons from the violent, the shoddy and the pseudo-tough, and from having their feelings hurt or hardened over.

- ◆ Help to make other men available for your son to learn from and be supported by, especially from 14 onwards.

- ◆ Teach your kids that sex is good, but special. Guard them from cheap and exploitative media and situations.

- ◆ If you are separated from the mother, don't disappear from your kids' lives.

- ◆ If your marriage is in trouble, your kids need you to address this. Don't just endure – get help or talk to someone you respect about how to change things. Don't walk away from it just because it's sometimes hard. Good marriages are achieved, they don't just happen.

Chapter 8

Making

School Good

for Boys

Each morning, if the weather was fine, the man used to walk his six-year-old son to school. They lived in a quiet village, and it was a beautiful country lane that led to the school. The boy would skip and run about, pointing out birds, insect life, ripening blackberries. As they drew closer to the school, though, a curious change always came over the boy. A change that saddened the father, for he knew what it was. The boy's voice deepened, his shoulders tensed up, his face got serious. He was putting on the armour that all males (in this culture) feel they must wear.

For the last 15 years I have worked with teachers across the globe, with the goal of making school better for boys. I have done this in places as diverse as Boulder and Leeds, Beijing and Capetown, Brazil and Singapore. Everywhere I hear the same message from teachers: the boys don't live up to their potential. They don't have any aspirations.

They get aggressive. They think it's cool to be a fool. The girls are racing ahead, the boys are losing the plot.

Girls racing ahead is not a problem to me: it's a tribute to the efforts educators have made to raise girls' aspirations and unleash their abilities. But boys are doing badly not just compared to girls, but to themselves, to what we know they could do if they tried, or got the right kind of help. Several reasons for this have been identified as significant.

- Boys develop at a different rate from girls. Largely this means they are slower in language, fine motor skills (such as handwriting) and social learning. It's likely they need to start school up to a year later, and move through school being slightly older than their classmates in order to keep pace with girls.

- Men have disappeared from teaching, especially primary school teaching, so boys don't see learning as a masculine activity.

- Boys with absent or busy fathers don't aspire to be like Dad. They are governed by their peer group instead. The peer group, unfortunately, is a rather stupid animal that doesn't value learning.

- The way school is structured seems poorly designed for boys, for whom it does not come naturally to sit very still, be quiet, learn passively, or do a lot of fine book work without much movement or hands-on practical work.

- And school often lacks the close-up mentoring and one-to-one help that even so-called 'primitive' societies were smart enough to provide.

- Finally, the emotional environment of boy culture in schools is often intimidating and negative. It is bullying and disparaging, and discourages risk-taking or creative behaviour.

Professor Ken Rigby, an Australian expert on bullying, has found that one in five boys gets bullied at school at least once a week. A boy who has had a gentle and coopera-tive start in life at home may find that to be accepted he has to put on macho pretensions, act mean, disparage girls and even join in acts of bullying.

Rigby describes the pattern in which the boy who is not academically bright (or is not helped to be so) becomes humiliated and angered in the classroom, and recovers his status by bullying others in the playground. Most men remember this from their boyhood; it even happens regularly on *The Simpsons*. Professor Rigby stresses the need for a non-blame approach that does not make boys angrier still. This by no means implies being soft on bullying. Research on effective school programmes has shown that every instance must be confronted, and the playground be made a safe place by teacher presence. The difference is that the problem is solved, and the needs of individual boys resolved so that they can move beyond needing to bully.

Rigby believes that the cold and uncaring nature of staff–student interaction contributes to the bullying atmosphere in a school. If the staff bully the children, they usually bully other children. The head and the teachers set the tone for the school. *Where friendly and warm interactions are offered by the staff, the school becomes a warmer and safer place. Where every boy feels successful, he will not see a need to take out in the playground the frustrations he experiences in class.*

The patterns of violence are very predictable in boys' lives. It's known that men who hit their wives or children, or who end up in prison for habitual violence, can easily be identified as early as the second year of primary school. Another recent study found that a high proportion of boys who behaved aggressively in primary school went on to become drunk drivers. *If we can predict these things, we can stop them happening.*

> **Men who ended up in prison were easily diagnosable by mid-primary school.**

Sport: a disaster area for body and soul

Sport often harms those who play it. In a 1994 rugby final between two prestigious schools in Queensland, Australia, a young man threw a punch at an opposing player. The other boy hit back, striking the side of the first player's head. The boy died from the punch. The teams had been under enormous pressure to win at all costs. The honour of the school and a disproportionate amount of attention had been loaded on to what should have been just a game. We know that boys' testosterone levels leap up in these situations and that they are prone to more aggressive behaviour.

Some coaches today urge boys in contact sports to hit and hurt as long as they can get away with it. Australian academic Dr Peter West believes that sport is one of the primary sources of shaping a defective masculine image: arrogant, elitist, violent, unfeeling, individualistic, competitive and less than fully human. Also, many children now sustain sports injuries, through overtraining or stress in competing, that affect them for life. Many parents now feel ambivalent about sport because of its psychological dangers, as well as its physical ones. Yet sport can be a positive influence in a boy's life, given the right conditions. School sport has to be adapted to serve the needs of children. It should be fun, inclusive, varied to suit all abilities, with only enough competition to create challenge. It should emphasise character, teamwork, pleasure of mastery and a sense of achieving personal best. It is a huge part of boyhood, so we have to get it right.

Seven steps to school reform

From worldwide research the following seven measures have emerged as the most urgent to take in making school good for boys.

1. Male teachers available at all levels of schooling

Men have disappeared from the teaching profession, especially in primary schools. Better pay, some positive recruitment, and less paranoia about sexual abuse are needed to reverse this

Some US school districts now legislate that all boys (and girls) have access to at least one in three teachers being male during their primary years. At the same time, we need more women teachers in senior positions, where they are still underrepresented.

Be wary, though, of recruiting men just because they are men. The best teacher is the person, regardless of gender, who has the personal qualities needed (see point 5 below).

2. A change in the role of male head teachers

If the head teacher is a man, and perhaps the only man in the school, it is important that he is accessible for and interactive with the children. He should not be remote, hidden behind administrative roles or continually taken away from school by other demands. Like it or not, he is a father figure and needs to be a good one.

3. More boyish modes of learning

Many school learning requirements are female orientated. Schools require and reward quiet, cooperative, verbal, fine motor, indoor, artistic and passive kinds of activity. We know that boys develop their fine motor skills more slowly than girls in early primary school – up to a year later in most instances. Boys feel stupid and awkward if expected to produce the same kind of work at the same age. With few exceptions, girls take to education more easily. Boys often have difficulty fitting into a classroom regime and carrying out classroom activities.

Education for boys needs to emphasise movement, vigour and going beyond four walls. They need more exciting or natural activity, which utilises male qualities instead of repressing them. This should not be limited to sport but extended to science, art, music, reading and maths. Many of these changes would benefit girls, too.

4. Releasing women teachers from the need to fight with problem boys

As discussed earlier, many problems of boys, especially violence and misbehaviour, can be attibuted to father hunger. By misbehaving, boys and young men are showing their need to be engaged, valued and disciplined by strong, loving male figures.

Female teachers often have horrendous, fruitless struggles with high-need boys, who have little respect for women and whose disruption prevents the whole class from learning. Even the most effective and experienced female teachers have told me they feel the boys are needing – virtually asking for – something they cannot give. They can achieve a truce, but still feel that these boys and young men need something more.

Women teachers should not have to struggle continually with boys who need something they cannot provide. Caring but strong mentors should be provided for troubled boys. This should not be just punitive attention, but preventive and long-term involvement aimed at giving them a positive masculine self-image.

5. Training of male teachers in the mentor role

Boys need men, but not just any men. Research by Dr Peter Downes for the Secondary Heads Association found that four qualities made for the best teacher. In order of importance, they needed to be friendly, focused, fun and firm. Boys learnt best from a man who was definitely in charge, but not mean or competitive, who was positive and well organised. They did not like a teacher who was one of the boys. And they would not learn unless they felt the teacher liked them.

> **The best teachers are friendly, focused, fun and firm.**

Male teachers may be quite poor role models if they have never received the mentoring they now need to impart. Special training is needed, particularly in the following areas:

- Counselling and conflict resolution.

- Understanding how boys lacking affection will often develop aggression as a substitute.

- The hero-or-villain dynamic in young men: how to redirect energies in constructive ways.

- Tough love confronting skills: how to teach thinking and problem-solving instead of using intimidation as a means of discipline.

6. Use of male–female teaching teams

Many boys and girls have never seen men and women working together and doing so successfully. School can be a great place for them to see this.

7. Gender equity programmes for boys too

Many good feminist teachers manage to be committed to the advancement of girls while supporting and encouraging boys as well. Yet this is not always the case. Mothers have told me that they feel their sons as young as kindergarten age are being made to feel inferior, just for being boys. While boys can be a problem, they do not wilfully choose to be difficult, lacking in social skills or aggressive. Boys get trapped, just as much as girls do, in low self-esteem and maladaptive behaviour. The difference is that their ways of showing this are more of a problem to others. Some feminist teachers would say, 'More attention for boys? Why should they get any more special attention?' But the fact is, if we want to solve the problems, we have to work from both ends. Most girls will want to know boys, will marry men and work with men. Things won't improve for girls unless boys are helped to make the corresponding changes.

Specific programmes for boys, run by male-affirming men and women, are needed to equip boys with the skills to stay alive and be competent socially, at school, at work, as husbands and as fathers. Boys need to learn fathering and the care of younger children throughout their schooling. Peer support and cross-age tutoring are good examples. Boys themselves appreciate the programmes and there are measurable benefits to behaviour.

To our pleasure and relief the reaction from teachers to all seven of these ideas has been overwhelmingly positive. They have told us, 'Yes, this accurately describes what has been missing. We do have to do something about boys, to complement what is starting to happen with girls. Thank goodness we now have some possible answers.'

Rather than endlessly playing 'more disadvantaged than thou' between the genders, we can recognise that boys and girls need different kinds of help. By treating all students the same, schools at present aren't being fair to either gender. Implementing just a few of these measures would create an improvement in the lot of boys, and before long would be bringing a better kind of young man out into the wider society.

In a nutshell

School can often be a place of fear and failure for boys. We can make school more boy-friendly in the following ways:

♦ Making the playground environment safer by instituting anti-bullying programmes and increasing the warmth, involvement and friendliness of teachers.

♦ Recruiting more of the right kind of men, especially into primary education.

♦ Stopping over-competitiveness in sport, and reinventing sport for enjoyment, self-development and exercise, not for the glory of the few.

♦ Helping teachers develop a mentoring role in boys' emotional development (so that school is an extension of family, and the 'whole boy' is the focus and aim).

Chapter 9

Finding a Job with Heart

Men love to work. If you drive through some suburbs late in the evening, you will always see garage lights on. Inside, groups of men labour over old cars, lovingly modifying, repairing and maintaining them late into the night. Others are busy building furniture in their workshops or working with metal and wood. These are mostly men who have worked hard all day in uninteresting jobs but who, with passion and intelligence, apply themselves at night-time to their real interests. Among the middle classes, the focus shifts to renovating – that endless fixing-up of our dwellings that seems to fill the years from 25 to 50 before we give up and slide downhill again, Visitors to the UK are struck by how many exotic and weird hobbies – from electric trains to orchids, ferret breeding to Shakespearean acting – seem to draw men out from the ordinariness of their daytime lives. We are the most creative creatures on

Earth, at our best and happiest when making our world better with our brains and hands.

Comradeship

In her remarkable book *The Continuum Concept*, Jean Liedloff tells of watching a group of Indian men dragging a heavy dugout canoe up a series of waterfalls in the Amazon rainforest. It takes hours. Suddenly, as they grunt their way up the last section, one man slips badly and the heavy canoe slams against the others and is shot by the force of the water hundreds of yards back down the cascade. To her amazement, the men roar with laughter, though several are cut and bruised and hours of time has been wasted. Still chuckling and teasing each other, they climb down the slippery rocks to start all over again. Liedloff marvels at the resilient spirit of these people, at the attitude they all seem to share, and wonders how such optimism is trained into their children.

Hard physical work comes naturally to men. Yet it is seen now as something lowly and degrading. D. H. Lawrence described how, in the industrial heartland of England, the men working in the coal mines took satisfaction and found comradeship in their work, and were proud of being good providers. Then schooling was introduced and, rather than working with their fathers, the boys began going to school. There they were taught by white-collared teachers that their fathers' world – the sweaty, difficult world of physical labour – was demeaning and that they should, through education, rise to a 'higher' world. Today we don't want to earn our living through sweat, but something is lost when we never share the companionship and pride of hard physical work.

Fit to be tied

In 1979 I applied for a Churchill Fellowship in the faint hope of being able to study in the USA. I was granted an interview. At the time I was 24, idealistic, still very much a hippy, rebellious and socially awkward. Minutes before the interview, I suddenly thought about what to wear. I called into a neighbour's house, borrowed a suit and tie, went to the interview and won the fellowship. I was lucky – it was a small town, and several of the interview panel knew my work, but without the tie, I don't think I would have qualified.

I borrowed a tie from a friend down the road... and won the fellowship.

A tie symbolises something very profound – a willingness to fit in or to submit. Every day outside any courthouse you will see people standing in suits and ties who look like they have never dressed that way before in their lives. No one is fooled by this. Everyone – the judges, the lawyers, the suit-wearers themselves – knows that this is a ruse to make the defendant look like a respectable person. But the gesture is important. It says,

'See, I am willing to go through the motions. I will be a good boy.'

At work a tie says, 'I am willing to put up with this discomfort, and therefore I am willing to put up with other indignities and constraints to get and keep this job. (Can I polish your boots with my tie?)' It's important to see a tie for what it is. It's a slave collar.

Class is a funny thing. Many men have discovered too late that rising in the class hierarchy does not make you freer. If you are a blue-collar worker, the company wants your body, but your soul is usually your own. A white-collar worker is supposed to hand over his spirit as well. There's a scene in the Australian film *The Fringe Dwellers*, where the Aboriginal men sit together making jokes about the poor white man spending his weekends mowing the lawn and washing the car. The Aboriginals are poor and at the bottom of the heap, but they at least feel freer than Whitey!

It's not just the tie: a whole uniform goes with it. The popular term for the men who attend to the boring details of the business world is 'suits'. Richard Gere, as the millionaire in *Pretty Woman*, strikes a deal and leaves the details to 'the suits' to tidy up. Suits (and the men who wear them) are all about a lack of individuality.

Ride the commuter planes and trains into cities any morning at 7 a.m. or late in the evening and you will be amazed at the herds of look-alike, grey-faced men, moving endlessly to and fro across the country in the dreadful

THE DEMON

WHEN I AWOKE THIS MORNING
EXHAUSTED FROM MY REST
A DEMON DARK AND TERRIBLE
WAS SITTING ON MY CHEST.

HE PINNED ME TO THE MATTRESS
AND SEIZED ME BY THE HEAD
HE PRESSED HIS KNEES AGAINST MY HEART
AND OVERTURNED THE BED.

HE DRAGGED ME TO THE MIRROR
AND SHOWED ME MY DISGRACE
THEN TOOK A RAZOR IN HIS CLAW
AND DRAGGED IT DOWN MY FACE

SOME FADED RAGS HE BOUND AROUND
MY SHOULDERS AND MY HIPS
AND POURED A CUP OF STEAMING MUCK
BETWEEN MY FADED LIPS

AND THEN HE TOOK THOSE WILTED LIPS
AND IN HIS EVIL STYLE
HE PARALYSED THE CORNERS UP
INTO A PLEASANT SMILE

A MASTERPIECE IN WICKEDNESS
THIS LAST SADISTIC JOKE
HE SENDS ME OUT INTO THE WORLD
A SMILING SORT OF BLOKE.

lifestyle of the executive. They might be flying business class and be first off the plane, into the club lounges, but no one could envy them. They are privileged eunuchs, leading a dry and joyless life.

Beware the mortgage trap

How does this all happen? How do intelligent men become enslaved? After all, no one forces us to compete in the rat race. Our system has one outstanding way of holding men in place – it's called a mortgage. A mortgage is a good idea gone wrong. It isn't the invention of bankers. The idea of owing for a lifetime has a long tradition. The feasters at a New Guinean wedding, for example, consume so many pigs and yams that a young man will spend his life repaying the debt. Similarly, Amish people in the USA will gather in their hundreds to build a large, beautiful barn in a single day, which will set up a newlywed couple for a lifetime of farming. The young couple will in turn help out at many other barn-raisings in the course of their lifetime. This is a system of mutual support, with a mutual obligation, which has kept the Amish safe, prosperous, recession-proof and with low divorce rates for several centuries.

The mortgage system allows you to have a house or apartment from the start of your adult life and to spend your life paying for it. Your obligation is not to people but to institutions. (Lose your job, fail to pay and faceless institutions will throw you out.) When you go for that vital interview at the bank (wearing your tie, of course) you walk out with £100,000. It's a miracle! But something else happens, something they don't tell you about. You leave a testicle behind. The bank manager keeps it in a jar in his safe, along with all the others. If ever in your life you get the urge to do something risky, exciting, different or adventurous, chances are you will not because you won't have the balls to do it.

Somehow, to be a free man, you have to escape this trap. You could live in the country where houses cost less. You could stop competing with your neighbours and drive the oldest car in your street. You could give your children more of your time, instead of a private school education. You could take a year off and just think it all over. Greed – buying and owning more and more stuff – is killing the world we live in, and it's killing you too. Yet it is the tune our government and our economy wants you to dance to. Even reducing this, claiming back some of your money and time, you can be a freer man.

Putting the heart back into work

It isn't the fact of working but the lack of meaning in that work that is the problem. If you do a job that lacks heart, it will kill you. The strongest predictor of life expectancy in a man – greater than diet, lifestyle or income – is whether he likes his job.

Our ancestors laughed as they worked and sang; they enjoyed the thrill of the hunt, the steady teamwork of searching for food plants, or the discovery of a honey-filled tree. Watch any documentary or archival footage of preliterate people and you will see this clearly. Life was often hard but it was rarely without laughter. In time, though, cultures evolved away from the forest and the coast and into the village and the town. We did the work that others decided, and it became a grind increasingly repetitive. It was a numbing of human senses and a subjugation of ourselves beneath the need just to survive. Today, work has become more comfortable but not more fulfilling. It's still a separate compartment in life – something you tolerate in exchange for 'real' living in the time left over from getting to your job, doing your job and recovering from your job. Work today drives an unhealthy wedge into the very core of our life. The time has come to heal it.

Most people today do work they do not much like, often in jobs that are beneath them. When I was a kid at school, we had 'career guidance'. Its ostensible aim was to help you find something you liked to do. But underneath it all we dimly sensed the real purpose. Since you had to work to purchase the good life, the aim was just to find the best paying job you could *tolerate*.

We all too easily pass this on to our kids. 'Get good grades, your future depends on it.' Yet the purpose of adolescence is to find what you really love to do. Once you find it, you must learn to do it well enough so that it will feed you. You will either be happy, or rich and happy. The aim is to have work that makes you jump out of bed in the morning, keen to get started. This is not so hard as you might have been led to believe.

The eight levels of fulfilling work

Below are eight criteria for assessing your working life. If you achieve any one of these, you deserve to feel good. If you feel bored and stuck in your work, then you are ready to move to the next stage. These criteria are not designed for comparing yourself to others. They are measures of individual heroism. A brain-injured man learning to clean his own backside can show more courage than a corporate high-flyer awarding himself a pay-rise.

1. Do you do your share?

This begins early. Even a three-year-old can and should contribute around the house. You can be an unemployed teenager living at home and still add to the well-being of your household. Perhaps you care for younger children, cook meals, do odd jobs round the house or grow food in a garden. You can feel proud that you contribute as well as receive. (It is over-consumption that has led to so much inequality and suffering, terrorism and war. What we need is more people who can simply carry their own weight.)

2. Can you support yourself?

If you have a job or earn an income of some kind, you are not drawing on the resources of the nation. These resources can be used instead to care for others who aren't able to support themselves. You are a plus to society. If achieving this second step is all you ever do, you are an asset.

3. Is your job one that allows you to improve the lives of others?

Many unglamorous jobs, such as bus driving, shopkeeping or reception work have an important daily impact on hundreds of people. By realising that your real work is the contact you make with people, and by doing so in a friendly, interested way (not just carrying out the mechanics of your task), you can have a positive effect on those you deal with and the people they deal with in turn.

> *It isn't enough to be successful; you have to ask yourself successful at what?*

4. Are you a provider for others?

Even if you have a job that is very routine, supporting others is an achievement. Partner, children and family can benefit and get a good start under the umbrella created by your being the provider. You are a life-giver.

5. Does your work provide an infrastructure for the work of others?

Does your job create other jobs, give leadership and structure, opportunity and growth to other people? Your work or small business may provide a niche for others that otherwise might not have existed.

6. Do you train and develop other people, enhancing their lives and futures?

Everyone in the workplace can continue to learn and grow. We all need mentors and parent figures in the workplace, not just bosses. We need men and women who have our interests at heart. Sit down and write out the qualities of the kind of boss you would like to work for. Then see if you can match up to these qualities. Being a mentor to others can be the most satisfying aspect of any job.

7. Does your work help protect the Earth, its people and its life?

Doctors have an ancient rule: at least, do no harm. If we all applied this in our jobs, it would be interesting. For instance, you might make a good living distributing a farm chemical that is dangerous but kept in use through powerful lobbying. Doing this would not be illegal, but clearly (like the plumbers at Auschwitz, say) you are part of something fundamentally bad. Would a caring shop-keeper refuse to sell cigarettes to anyone? A film-maker needs to ask, what kind of movies does the world need?

The ad man, what kind of ads? A journalist, what kind of news items? A real man has to look at these questions. It isn't enough just to be successful. You have to ask, successful at what?

8. Does your work use your innate abilities and talents so that it is unique and powerful in its effect on the world?

Some men know how to teach children, others can heal pain, carve sculptures, make violins, ride a wave, kick a ball, lay cement, design glorious buildings, make new laws. When your job is also your creativity brought to life, you do wonderful work.

Every man has creative activity coiled up inside him. How can you tell? You will know – an unexpressed urge will actually hurt you if it isn't let out. Begin in a small way and see where it leads.

Same job, different attitude

Realistically, for many men, the trick is finding the heart in the work you already do. Think about your job. How would you go about removing the façade that is traditionally built up in your line of work so that you can be more of the real you? I recently saw an estate agent manage the sale of a house for an old lady whose husband lay dying in hospital. She did this with such care that everyone, buyer and seller, became friends and went to the funeral together. I have a friend who is Australia's top orthodontist. He tells a quarter of the people who walk through his door that they don't need his services. They would be wasting their money. I once watched a shop assistant, a young man of about 20, so gentle and tender in his handling of a confused old lady that it brought tears to my eyes. These people are different from the norm, and they transform the banal situation into magic. They have the grace that comes from some inner sense of what matters.

I don't think all work can be converted in this way. Some basically negative occupations, like politics as it is currently practised, that involve, say, environmental damage or dishonest selling, breed a paranoia that twists in on itself, however much the man doing it denies that he gives a damn. Like St Paul on the road to Damascus, there comes a time to say, 'I quit'.

Capitalism has outlasted communism, but that doesn't mean it actually works. In fact – as several very well-qualified economists, from E. F. Schumacher to J. K. Galbraith, have pointed out – it depends on constant, cancer-like growth, which will make the world unliveable. If mainstream men keep doing what they are doing, earning and spending more and more, the world will simply choke to death. When mainstream men can learn to live with less, and derive their pleasure from doing and being instead of from owning, it might be possible to have a post-capitalist economy that actually works – and is lots more fun to live in.

Retirement: an insult and a waste

Years ago I heard David Mowaljarlai, a Kimberley Aboriginal elder, speaking about the life cycle of a man in traditional society. One of the older (white) men present asked whether an Aboriginal elder ever retired. David smiled and described the ceremony his people would conduct each year, in which the leader of a clan would have to climb to the top of a pole placed in the ground, thus proving that he was still strong enough to lead. I thought at the time how subtle a device this was, since most people would assume that the old man would want to stay as leader. And yet an old man would actually have a choice whether he made it to the top of the pole or not: 'Damn! I guess I just can't make it this year.'

Retirement is a source of some pain and ambivalence among many men. Perhaps this was the questioner's thought too as he asked, 'What then?'

Mowaljarlai searched in his mind for the right word. 'I don't know what you call it in English. The old fella, he becomes no longer the leader, he's the manual.'

For a moment I thought he meant manual labour. I envisaged a disgraced elder cleaning up around the camp.

People looked blank. Mowaljarlai tried to explain. 'You know, like the book you get with your car.'

Someone caught on. 'Oh, the instruction book.'

'Yes,' said Mowaljarlai. 'When the new leader, he comes across something he can't handle, he hasn't seen before, he goes and consults the manual.'

In American factories many older managers and foremen were fired in the 1980s, as accountants took over and ran things by the bottom line. But things started to go wrong. Soon, according to *In Search of Excellence* author Tom Peters, these old men were brought back, on high pay and short hours, to walk around the factories and look things over. They had the sixth sense, the subtle knowledge, to tell when a huge and expensive machine was about to malfunction, or an interpersonal problem was developing to crisis point. They could act before the problem *was* a problem because they knew how to read the signs. There is no substitute, you see, for experience.

In a nutshell

♦ Burn your tie or use it to tie up the tomato plants.

♦ Either find a job you can believe in or find something to believe in about your job.

♦ If you're a boss, realise that you are a father figure. You are there to nourish and care for your people so that they can do their jobs.

♦ Keep working towards the goal of having work that uses the most creative and unique things about you in ways that improve the life of the world. The intersection of your individual abilities and the world's needs is a very happy place to be.

♦ Love, fun and idealism have as much place at work as in any other aspect of life.

♦ If you must retire, don't retire from life. Become an elder. Above all, stay involved.

Don't burn your tie

Walker Feinlein, Professor of Textile Anthropology at the University of Hobart in Tasmania, strongly counsels against burning your tie in a fit of masculinist fervour. Bra-burning in the 1960s was largely a media creation, he explained, arising out of an accident with a faulty cigarette lighter. Alternative uses for ties include using them to stake the tomato plants, throwing a couple in the car boot for use as an emergency fan belt, or tying several ties together to create a colorful drum strap for those all-night sessions.

Other voices

Yes, I think...men have become enslaved. Possibly it's the industrialisation process. They've become removed from Nature, which kept them connected to feelings. Zorba the Greek is not easily found amongst contemporary men. *(Laughs)* They seem to be enslaved and somewhat castrated, I think, and the fact that men have to get up in the morning and go off to work (this is how it was traditionally)...I used to see my father do this: get up at 5.30 a.m., go off to a cold meatworks, come home late, exhausted, every day of his life. He just wasn't in the race; he didn't have a chance in many ways. He had to be tough; he wasn't allowed to have those feelings.

And I think this has suited women to some extent too, or a lot of women I mean, just as feminism seemed to women to be throwing off the role that was allotted to them, I think this has yet to happen to men. Men are carrying so much expectation and misunderstanding. It hasn't been easy to be a male through the feminist years because to be constantly told that all men are rapists and all men are exploitative, and all men are pigs, and blah blah blah...while one recognises the truth in part of that, it's not good, it doesn't help men at all, it's made men retreat. Men have lost their nerve a bit, as they need to, but I just hope it goes on and they rise up a bit against – not women, because they need to love women and to care for women, women aren't the enemy. Maybe it's a sort of capitalism, maybe it's consumerism; maybe it's all these things, that 'the system', as they say, has enslaved men. They've been made into a 'work unit', an economic unit, they have to keep earning all this money. *(Caroline adds: And keep this system going which, as you pointed out earlier, really isn't serving us terribly well, it would seem now, and that's heartbreaking.)*

It's a terrible thing...If it was serving us well, if we had marvellous schools and it was all a bit more humanistic, and fulfilling, then, well, let's work hard. But all this hard work, and distress, and this debt – for what? So you can watch some cheap video, and eat junk food, and look at your neighbourhood falling apart, and the shopping centre full of plastic signs and noise and carelessness? Men need to...I think men often define themselves in some way or feel connected to this world by their skills, their dexterity, the way they can make things and do things. They're becoming more useless, it seems, more enslaved, more trapped. They sit at desks, and they've got to look good – they've got to look so damn good now, and so neat and pressed, and the hair's got to be just right, and they've got to smell nice and stare at a screen all day. The regimentation is appalling, and what does this do to the human spirit? What is it doing to the spirit of man? If there be an essential male psyche or something, I imagine it's having a terrible effect.

Caroline: When do you get the fullest sense of being who you are? I like being in the dirt a bit, getting my hands dirty, or something like that. What about sex? I mean, why does no one mention sex when they're asked what they most like to do? That's an important thing I do. I like sex, I like eating, I like going to bed at night – those fundamental things. These are terribly central and important. I like gardening, I like digging a hole. I like to construct something, I like to paint...I think those things are sacred, and they are common to us all, I would think. Oh, and this other thing...I think that people are deprived somewhat by modern life; the chance to be of some clear value to the society or to a person, to save someone's life, or to pick someone off the road or to help them. You watch people in a country town if there's a bushfire. Everyone just leaps to get out and do a bit for each other, and it brings out this lovely vitality, and people discover all levels within themselves.

Michael Leunig, Australia's best-known cartoonist, interviewed by Caroline Jones

I am not a mechanism, an assembly of various sections.

And it is not because the mechanism is working wrongly that I am ill.

I am ill because of wounds to the soul, to the deep emotional self,

and the wounds to the soul take a long, long time, only time can help

and patience, and a certain difficult repentance

long, difficult repentance, realisation of life's mistake, and the freeing oneself

from the endless repetition of the mistake

which mankind at large has chosen to sanctify.

D.H. Lawrence, *Healing*

I have chosen to emphasise what I think is believed to be the most central source of men's alienation – the absence of a sense of abiding meaning or, as I prefer to say, vocation, in our lives.

Sam Keen, *Fire in the Belly*

Without work, all life goes rotten. But when work is soulless, life stifles and dies.

Albert Camus, French writer

Chapter 10

Real Male Friends

An Australian story. Two farmers stand in the dusty yard of an outback cattle station. One is a neighbour, come to say goodbye, the other is watching as the last of his furniture is loaded on to a truck. The farm looks bare – livestock gone, machinery sold. A teenage boy and girl stand by the car, the wife sits inside it, eyes averted.

The two men have farmed alongside each other for 30 years, fought wildfires, driven through the night with injured children, eaten thousands of meals, drunk gallons of coffee, and cared for each other's wives and kids as their own. They have shared good times and bad. Now, one is leaving, bankrupted. He will go to live in the city, where his wife will support them by cleaning motels.

'Well,' says the man. 'I'll be off then.'

'Yeah,' says the other. 'Thanks for coming over.'

'Look us up sometime.'

'Yeah, I reckon.'

And they climb into their vehicles and leave. And while their wives will correspond for years to come, these men will never exchange words again.

So much unspoken. So much that would help the healing to take place from this terrible turn of events. What pain would flow out if one was to say, 'Listen, you've been the best friend a bloke could want,' and looked the other straight in the eye as he said it. Or if they had spent some long evenings together with their wives, full of 'Remember whens...' punctuated by tears and easing laughter. If, instead of standing stiff-armed and choked, they could have had a long, strong hug from which to draw strength and assurance as they faced the hardship their futures would bring. The farmer leaving the land will not find the opportunity for any of these supports, comforts or appreciations. He will be a massive risk for suicide, alcoholism, cancer or accident, as he twists up inside to suppress the emotions his body feels.

Men, you see, don't have friends – at least not in those countries cursed with an Anglo-Saxon heritage. Instead we have 'mates' with whom we share a secret agreement on which subjects we never discuss. A subtle and elaborate code governs the humour, the put-downs, the ways in which serious feeling or vulnerability is deflected. All this is well known and often written about. So it's time to make a change.

Little boys start out warm and affectionate. You will see

them in the younger grades at school, arms about each other. And at this age they are still tender and kind to younger children, unfussed about being with girls and able to cry over a dead pet or a sad story. So what goes wrong? Let's find out.

Proving you're a man

We've already said that men are absent from the lives of little boys. So are older boys, since in our society we isolate each age group and expect them to mix only with same-age, same-sex children. This is an odd arrangement, since little boys love to be around older boys in every village and slum and tribe around the world. By comparison, the world of the little boy in primary school is a harsh and scary one because the older children have not been taught to nurture the younger ones, but rather to see them as competition for limited adult affection. The playground is violent and mean. It follows the law of the jungle – the kind of conditions portrayed in the book *Lord of the Flies*.

Paul Whyte, of the Sydney Men's Network in Australia, uses an exercise to help women understand what it is like to be a boy in the schoolyard culture. He asks them to imagine that membership of their gender depends on being able *to physically defend themselves against others of their gender*. Imagine, for a minute, if being a woman meant having to fight, physically, with any

> *Imagine if being a woman meant having to fight with any woman who came along.*

woman who came along and having to hold your ground against her. If you couldn't do this, you would be beaten and you would be accused of not being a woman. This is life for many boys at school. Verbal attack, if not actual violence, is an ever-present threat, and proving yourself adequate through physical strength is a continual issue. This portrayal certainly describes my childhood. How about yours?

Proving you're not gay

Because their masculinity is not taught or proactively developed by the men of the community, boys feel a strong need to prove their masculinity. Most parents will notice how their son drops his voice to a deeper pitch when his friends are around, or refuses to kiss his baby sister goodnight if a friend is visiting.

Into this already volatile situation, especially as puberty arrives, comes a strange twist. The existence of homosexuality as a biological fact in the human race, combined with many people's inability to be comfortable with this variation in type, means that the dread of being thought gay hangs over the head of any boy who is different in any way from the norm. The risk is great, and varies from being rejected, ridiculed, beaten, or even killed, depending on the severity of the culture. Our non-acceptance of gays is tough on a youngster experiencing homosexual leanings, but it also exacts a severe price on every straight young man. It leads to the self-censoring of any kind of warmth, creativity, affection or emotionality among the whole male gender. A boy thinks, 'If I'm not macho, I might be seen to be gay.' Children may exhibit this fear even when they are not aware of what being gay means. They just know it's something not to be.

When we oppress gay people, we oppress ourselves as well. No one feels free to be themselves.

The scourge of competition

Competitiveness as a personality trait stems from compulsively searching for approval that never comes. Even winning, as many top athletes find, is not enough. Yet, given adequate approval from their mentors, boys and men do not have this compulsion to impress. They settle down to learning for its own sake, less concerned with being biggest and best. There are parts of the world where competition simply does not exist. Native American children often help each other to take tests, for example, and Balinese people are gloriously creative and artistic without any sense of one being better than another.

Size is everything

Everyone agreed that condoms were a great idea, except for one thing: while men came in different sizes, condoms came only in one standard size. Manufacturers had figured out early that no self-respecting man would walk into a chemist's shop and ask for a packet of small condoms.

The conversation turned quiet at this point as each person made their own inner reflections. Finally someone hit on an answer. The smallest size could be called large! What about the larger sizes? The atmosphere became ribald at this stage. It was finally agreed, after many suggestions, that there should be three sizes of condom: large, huge and oh my God!

Adapted from a story in the *Whole Earth Review*

Competition is a continual undercurrent of men's lives. One man wrote to me:

I notice when I sit down in a public place, beside a swimming pool or in a park, I relax and feel good if there is no one else around. If another man arrives, I first run a check that he is no physical threat, that he is not about to mug me. No one has ever mugged me or hurt me since childhood, but the feeling still lives. [Women understand this reflex, albeit for different reasons.] Then I get to assessing whether he is stronger, has better clothes, or is more athletic. If he is with a woman, I look for signs that she doesn't really like him. If the car park is within view, I check out his car for comparison with my own. Even if he is friendly and a conversation starts, I have to fight the urge to mention my achievements, what an important person I am – to subtly start winning the contest. The inner competition never stops. I seem caught in a basically hostile and insecure obsession with comparisons.

I am now retraining myself to change this damaging and isolating pattern. I am teaching myself to see other men as brothers, with good things to give and to receive. I have always felt this warmth and friendliness towards women, but why not men too? This is leading to a huge change in attitude and a huge boost in my enjoyment of half the human race.

Boys who are denied appropriate physical affection and praise from their father or other males while growing up seem to have difficulty forming male friendships. In fact, they have a huge distrust of other men. You can see these men at any football game or boxing match. They seem to thrive on the violent aspects of male contact, while distancing themselves from any form of intimacy. Luckily, this twentieth-century phenomenon is passing, and men today are much more likely and able to hug or give praise to each other.

When men are freely allowed to experience the care and support of other men, they begin to question competition in our society. This questioning engenders a willingness to engage in more service-orientated projects and activities whose aim is to nurture and protect others. Here lies the potential for a whole different kind of man.

Beyond competition

The indigenous Xervante people of northern Brazil divide manhood into eight stages of growth. These peer groups stay very close throughout life, and they are also assisted and tutored by those in the group higher up in the sequence. Each year the Xervante hold running races for each age group in turn. These races look like a contest but they are not. When a runner falters or trips, the others pick him up and run with him. The group always finishes as a pack.

In fact, it's not a race at all in the sense we understand it, though everyone puts in a huge effort. It's a celebration of manhood, an expression of surplus vitality. This is a culture that has survived thousands of years by cooperation. They don't have to prove they are men – they celebrate that they are men.

Writer Marvin Allen says it beautifully: 'I defy anyone,

anywhere in the world, to prove that they're a man.' In fact, it's a ridiculous concept. Women wouldn't entertain the concept of proving they are women.

Friends make life infinitely more worth living. They help to spend your time well. They show you that you belong and can be cared about. Perhaps this is why men traditionally cook at barbecues. It's a declaration that men can feed you too. If you don't believe this, listen to the banter that takes place between men and women over the quality of the burgers and sausages.

A man who lacks a network of friends is seriously impaired in living his life. Friends alleviate the neurotic over-dependence on a wife or girlfriend for every emotional need. If a man going through a rough time gets help from his friends as well as his partner, the burden is shared. If his problems are with his partner (as they often are), his friends can help him through, talk sense into him, stop him from acting stupidly and help him to release his grief.

A male-out: men supporting men in crisis

Some years ago, in a large government department in the city where I live, a man in his late forties was given a notice of dismissal. He had been a dedicated, professional worker, yet his boss did not have the guts to tell him personally. Instead, this man and several colleagues received a photocopied retrenchment letter and that was that.

The man became increasingly irrational and in his lunch break went out and purchased a gun, which he put in the boot of his car. He shredded a large number of work documents, and went home in an emotional state, greatly alarming his wife and young children.

Several friends conferred about what to do. They went to his house, taking food and sleeping bags, and spent the next couple of days living there, while his wife and children were sent elsewhere. They rostered themselves so that someone was always awake and with the man, who was too agitated to sleep very much. By the Sunday afternoon, after much talking, crying and holding, the man thanked his friends for stopping him from 'making an idiot' of himself and began to make concrete plans for his future. The friends monitored him closely; one stayed on at the house for two more days and checked that things were, in fact, going well. His family came back home a few days later, and his life has progressed well.

The friends knew somehow that this was their job – it was men's business. Male friends can do these things where wives and other women probably cannot. Other men know how you are feeling. Men understand the issues about being a hero/provider, which do not have a female equivalent. Sometimes only other men can help you learn about the ongoing process of being a man.

Communicating feelings

Millions of women complain about their husband's lack of feeling, his woodenness. Men themselves often feel numb and confused about what they really want.

Pop psychology books of the *Men Are from Mars, Women Are from Venus* genre tell us just to accept this. But what if men's inarticulateness simply comes from a lack of sharing opportunities with other men? If men talked to each other more, perhaps they'd understand themselves better. Perhaps with this practice they could better articulate to their wives what is going on for them. It seems entirely possible that only in the company of other men can men begin to activate their hearts. Writer and men's activist Michael Meade says that just as men's voices have a different tone, so do their feelings. We have more than enough feelings, but they are not the same as women's feelings. Once we gain a language for these, we have no trouble expressing ourselves.

The dehumanising of men

How many of you here are tall, rich, you know, successful, powerful, got an eight-inch dong, got hair on your chest, slender, muscular, always in control...has anybody...we've got one over here! Only man here!

There's a new definition of a man here, and it

> has at least – at least – as much emphasis on
> loving and nurturing, as on providing and
> protecting.
>
> **Marvin Allen**

Men get set up in a serious double bind by society as a whole. They are asked, especially of late, to be more intimate and more sensitive. However, they are still coached in the possibility of being sent to war, still expected to be tough when needed. We don't actually want men who are weaker, just men who can shift between tough and tender as the situation requires, which is a considerable skill. A woman at a conference summed this up very well:

> I have been married twice, and had several other
> relationships that ended badly. Like most
> women, I have always listened to men, but until
> today I never heard them. I have never heard
> men talk to other men with such depth and love.
> And I never imagined what it was like for men to
> live with the knowledge that they must be
> prepared to kill, or with the actual horror of
> battle. This weekend I feel like I have been in a
> room with giants. I thank you for letting me
> listen.

One writer described travelling with four friends in a car and coming across a serious accident scene. The men piled out of the car, stopped traffic, pulled injured people out of vehicles, staunched serious bleeding and did their best to comfort the family of two people who had been killed outright. It was a remote place, and three hours had passed before it was all over.

'What I would like to have seen,' the writer said later, 'was a newspaper headline reading: "Five men control their feelings in order to save lives in highway carnage".' He was pointing out that controlling one's feelings is a very valuable part of male make-up. It has great survival value, and all women, deep down, count on it. Also being able to let go of those feelings, when the time is right, is another matter entirely.

At a gathering of men

A group of men sits in an afternoon gathering, part of a larger conference on the family. Women have been asked not to attend this meeting. The atmosphere in the room is different from the other seminars of the day, slightly sombre, a little charged. A middle-aged woman who is lost puts her head round the door, immediately senses the atmosphere, mumbles an apology and disappears.

It's my job to lead this seminar. I sit quietly, getting comfortable with the room, settling down into my body.

When the time comes, I begin to speak and the group slowly warms up. Unlike the vitality and the slight sense of indignation you will often find in a gathering of women, in a men's group there is great reserve, even fear. This is lightened a little by banter and warmth from some of the older, more experienced men. As a man in my forties, I stand midway no longer as brash or superficially confident as I once was, and also aware of the depth of experience that lies in the room. So I speak first to the older men and thank them for coming. I acknowledge explicitly that they have lived longer and deeper lives than I have. I ask for their help to make the session a success. I also welcome younger men, and thank them for their freshness and energy. I hope they can do a better job when their time comes.

The discussion follows a kind of natural gravitational pull which, at this time in men's history, seems to be the way forward. We talk first about what is not working – rifts with fathers, painful experiences in marriage, parenthood, health. The invitation is for men to tell parts of their experience and simply listen to each other. One after another, men speak. As they speak, quietly and simply, eyes fill and men begin to cry. From time to time we break into smaller clusters of men, then return to share conclusions. It is hard to stop people talking. At the end, no one wants to leave. It is another hour after the appointed time before the last man shares a long hug with me and goes on his way.

There is a pressure inside men that has been building up for a very long time through a lack of really honest talk. It's nothing complicated just, 'How is your life going?' Yet this kind of conversation does not happen at a bar or the gym, or the Rotary Club or a church meeting. So the opportunity for a very natural and necessary part of men's soul development is missing from our lives. Imagine how tense women would become if they could never talk to other women. Understanding this, perhaps men's tension and numbness makes more sense. We've held back from each other for so long.

Grief

Grief expert Mal McKissock has said that when men shut down their feelings, it starts to kill them. A bereaved man is eight times more likely to die in the two-year period following bereavement. If a child in a family dies – a cot death, for instance – there is a 70 per cent likelihood that the parents' marriage will not survive the loss. We simply and urgently must provide a means for men to express their grief. McKissock explains that failing to grieve leads to a loss of passion in the whole of life. No one wants to stay married to a block of wood, so the marriage disintegrates. Wives and partners have their own pain, and are therefore unable to provide what is needed. McKissock believes that failing to feel one single emotion (in this case, sadness) leads to a shutdown in the full spectrum of feelings – anger, fear, warmth and love. This passion is what most men have lost, and is also what we stand to gain.

Crying is a simple physical act. When we cry our body produces its own healing endorphins that wash through our brain, healing the losses we've sustained. Once we've wept, we can breathe freely, see clearly, feel the love of others, and face the world again.

The better a man takes care of himself during these dark times, the sooner he passes through the dark night. The more damage and denial he does to himself, the longer he will take to heal, and the deeper will be the mistakes he makes along the way. More hearts will be broken in his attempts to heal his own broken heart.

A man once came to see me, who had lost his father through illness at the age of eight. His mother committed suicide two years later, and the children found her body when they came home from school. He and his younger brothers were split up and sent to various relatives and rarely saw each other. By the time I met him, he was a highly successful businessman, but was troubled by sudden rages, which had lost him a number of employees. He had two failed marriages and was just holding on in a third. By now he knew that the problem was in him, and was ready to talk. All he really needed to do was tell the story and express the grief that went with it – a simple, profound act that he had never done with anyone since childhood. As he told his story, softly and slowly, he would suddenly be overcome with great washes of tears and sobbing. I felt utterly helpless in the face of this terrible story, but in that helplessness I sat and gave my absolute attention, saying very little beyond encouraging him to continue. Gradually, the most extraordinary feeling of peace came into the room where we were sitting.

Fun and friendship

The other reason for having male friends is to have fun – the kind of fun that is noisy, energetic, affectionate, ribald, accepting and free.

> We called ourselves SPERM (the Society for the Protection and Encouragement of Righteous Manhood).
>
> **Sam Keen, *Fire in the Belly***

Some teenage boys near where I live did an unusual thing. They had enjoyed some camping trips on the banks of the Huon River, and decided they wanted to build a wooden boat and sail down the river. Since they were young men, rather than children, their parents gave the project their blessing. With the help of one of the fathers, they found a shed to work in, scrounged materials, worked weekends, saved money, and the boat gradually took shape.

Things did not always go smoothly between them. One young man often failed to match the monetary contribution of the others, and added to the insult by borrowing (and not returning) money from them for other purposes.

Since several of them had taken part-time jobs to raise funds, they were angry after a time and decided to confront him: 'You aren't pulling your weight. You're using us.'

Because of the bond that already existed between them, and the firm but unaggressive way they tackled him, he did not storm off. He thought it over, got a job and paid back what he owed. He gained in the character department.

Another of the young boat-builders had trouble with overbearing parents, who had high expectations of his doing brilliantly at school. The others noted his growing depression and consulted their parents about how to help. They decided simply to tell their friend up front: 'Listen, man, you only have to live with your parents for another year. Hang in there and finish school. Then your life's your own. You do what you want to do with your life. You can always live here in the boathouse.'

These were islands of seriousness in a sea of good times. Everyone's life is eased, stabilised and supported by such friendships. Why shouldn't all men, young and old, have such a safety net in their lives? It could avoid all kinds of disasters.

In a nutshell

♦ Weed out any kind of competition from your friendships, beyond the playful kind that makes sport more exciting.

♦ Stop trying to prove you're a man. Just be one.

♦ Be affectionate. Give straight compliments from time to time.

♦ Listen to your friends' problems without trying to minimise them or give advice.

♦ Join a men's group where men talk about their real lives and discuss painful topics as well as cheerful ones.

♦ Don't be afraid of grief and tears. You probably have a backlog already.

♦ Have fun with other men. Be noisy, wild and safe. Be proud of being male. Maintain a good network of friends.

Chapter 11

The Wild Spirit of Man

This chapter looks at three of the deeper concepts of men's spiritual development. These are initiation, the wild man and the time of Ashes.

For this is the journey that men make. To find themselves. If they fail in this, it doesn't matter what else they find.

James A. Michener, *The Fires of Spring*

Religion, spirit and man

Throughout history, all the peoples of the Earth have practised some kind of religion. In fact, it has always been a central force in their lives. The caves of Lascaux, with their beautiful animal paintings, are our earliest records of masculine ritual. In many societies in pre-history (including the Aboriginal culture of Australia, where I live), religious practices took up more than 70 per cent of the time and energy of the older men and women. We have either to conclude that these people were primitive, superstitious and therefore stupid, or that there was a purpose and life-supporting function in these activities, even though we may only dimly understand what that could be.

Our logical minds are limited, they were designed for simple tasks, not for understanding the universe. Yet, at the same time, we can sense a unity and wholeness to creation which, when we are in tune with it, makes our lives flowing and unselfish, and gives us courage and purpose. Feeling connected to all that is around us, not separate, selfish or isolated, is the heart of spirituality.

Religion is our attempt to strengthen and maximise people's ability to be spiritual. In spite of the divisions, scams and bigotries that religion can foster, the forces of good – from working with prisoners on death row, to campaigning for world disarmament – have a strong religious component. And the most potent and effective men and women – from Nelson Mandela to the Dalai Lama to Aung San Suu Kyi – are those with religious underpinnings to their life.

Today we have very little ritual in our lives; we think it has no use. Yet even when we use the term 'empty ritual' we are acknowledging that ritual can also be full. Collective events, such as ceremonies and gatherings, are important ways to get our roots down into the nourishing depths of life so that we are not swept away like dead leaves into trivia and depression. For example, a wedding in some cultures lasts for many weeks. A British wedding, on the other hand, is over in several hours. Then there is the 10-minute Nevada version. No prizes for guessing which will carry more meaning. If people decided to dispense with funerals, it would be a devastating thing for the mental health of relatives and friends. It would say nothing mattered about this person's death, or their ever having lived. The inevitable outcome of this point of view is to commit suicide. Christening a baby, attending a bar mitzvah, getting married, celebrating a birthday, visiting a graveside...are all rituals that take us under the surface of life – they are a psychological means of going deeper, getting to the heart of things. A gravestone is not for the benefit of the dead person. It is an anchor point for the minds of the bereaved, to help them affirm that this person really lived. With this knowledge, they can hold that person's value and memory as active forces for health and empowerment as they live their own lives.

The brand of religion one chooses to pursue is not especially important. The differences between religions are only differences of style and technique. Christ, Buddha, Shiva and Mohammed would have got on just fine. In a sense, any spiritual path will do. Not to have some kind of spiritual practice in one's life, however, is a serious mistake.

I have treated many hundreds of patients.
Among those in the second half of life, that is to
say over 35, there has not been one whose
problem, in the last resort, was not that of
finding a religious outlook on life.

Carl Jung

Family isn't enough

Many men, if questioned, locate the purpose for their lives
in pursuing the well-being of their family. So it might
surprise you to learn that this is not enough. Altruistic as
it may sound, to make one's family all-important is spiri-
tually parasitic. Living through your wife is very bad for
you both. Making your children your purpose for living
puts an unbearable burden on them. Raising a family may
take up almost your whole life, yet it isn't the heart of your
existence because one day it will be over. You, and the
universe, are the only two concerns that last.

A poet's job is not to save the soul of a man, but
to make it worth saving.

James E. Fletcher, quoted in *Wingspan*

In *Fire in the Belly*, Sam Keen tells of being helped by an
older man friend while going through a painful divorce.
This man told him, 'There are two questions a man must
ask himself. The first is, "Where am I going?" The second

is, "Who will go with me?" If you ever get these questions in the wrong order, you are in trouble.' Most of us get the order wrong.

Learning from the past

'Where am I going?' is the critical question of our lives. 'Where have I come from?' might hold some of the answers. You know where you have come from: there is a trail running back behind you through the centuries, all the way to a Cro-Magnon hunter half a million years ago. You are alive and here today because he was wise, tough, skilful, nurturing and courageous enough to be able to form loving relationships, nurture children, work with the forces of nature and survive. (And his partner(s) were likewise.) You have the same superb capacities that he did. The problem is how to awaken them.

Ecology as a spiritual path

It has already been said (in chapter 9) that your ultimate job as a man is to preserve life. This doesn't just mean your little corner of life – your kids and your backyard. Living a life that makes ecological sense isn't just a practical challenge, but involves an inner change of orientation too. The biologist who goes out to study the rainforest from an objective point of view comes back changed by the experience. The nights under the massive forest canopy and the days peering into nature's mysteries have captured his soul. He changes from a dried-up 'nerd' to a passionate and newly balanced man. (Annie Dillard's Pulitzer prize-winning book *Pilgrim at Tinker Creek* is a good place to start if you wish to awaken this perception of nature. So is *Lord of the Rings*, for that matter – a book all about the fight between nature, community and industrialisation.)

There's every indication that ecology is becoming a new religion, especially for idealistic young people. It's equally possible, though, that the needs of our time will simply transform our existing religions into something more vibrant and purposeful, by turning more to nature and wildness and less to dogma and intellectual head-tripping. Ecologically aware forms of Christianity, Islam and Hinduism are currently emerging, and Buddhism is already a superbly ecological religion.

Many people are attracted to a more natural life, not just from 'save the Earth' concerns, but because they are pulled towards it by the wildness in their own nature. Indeed, there are many who would claim not to be religious at all, yet the wilderness and the ocean are already their spiritual homes. Surfers, mountaineers, hikers, fishermen are responding to this call. Even an old person growing roses is seeking the spiritual. The thirst for wildness is with us every day. The more artificial life becomes, the more people strive to redress the balance. Nature always offers the happiest way for humans. The closer modern man gets to inner and outer wildness, the better things will go.

This takes more than just sitting in a forest and smoking dope. Ancient cultures knew that to 'arrive' as a man in harmony with the outer world requires a long journey. It's an involved process requiring effort and care from parents and elders, lasting many years. It's not enough to eat sprouts and be groovy; serious disciplines and processes have to be gone through.

Initiation – the breakthrough to manhood

Once, when I was a young, gangling teenager, I was swimming in the ocean near my home when a rather beautiful young mother and two little children came down to the shore. One of the children threw some stones in the water. 'Be careful not to hit that man,' cried the mother. I looked about surprised – I hadn't known anyone else was in the water. Then I realised – she meant me. It made my day.

We believe being a man is a matter of size and age alone. The results of this are clear to see – boys in men's bodies everywhere you look. In centuries gone by becoming a man was a long, planned process. It required ritual and effort and the deliberate, active intervention of the whole community. This ritual and effort, although very diverse in their forms around the planet, were practised in every society, from Inuit to Zulu, by every race and in every time. It was the first thing anthropologists noticed when they visited cultures other than their own. It had a name. It was called initiation.

Kikuyu men in Kenya, to take just one example, would take the youngsters of a certain age away from the women, and the boys would go without food for three days. Then the older men would arrive and cut their veins to fill a bowl with blood, which the young men drank. Most of us shudder to hear this. What is this all about? Perhaps it tells the boys that men can nourish too. The boys are then fed, cared for, prepared for rituals and given intense attention by the older men. In the days that follow, the old men recount the creation myths, stories and songs that are part of being male in that culture. They charge the boys with responsibilities to the people and the land. The boys feel their connection beyond just family to all men who have lived in that place, and see themselves as a link in time and space that goes on into the future. Similar activities, separate and unknown to the boys, carry the girls into womanhood.

Initiatory journeys you might have made

Lacking initiation processes today, we often find ourselves drawn to create such experiences unconsciously. One night, while reading the work of Joseph Campbell, the renowned mythologist, I realised I had made at least one initiatory journey myself. I'm sure many men will recognise the pattern from their own youth. According to Campbell, the initiatory journey always has three steps:

1. A separation from home and family and all that is familiar.

2. A frightening, difficult, but exhilarating journey, helped along by unexpected hospitality from strangers and help from mystical allies. This enables you to face your vulnerability and break out of many youthful fears and neuroses.

3. Finally, a return home: the traveller apparently the same person, but forever changed.

When I was 17 I saw a poster on a university noticeboard, inviting young Australians to go alone and live in a Papua New Guinea village and experience Stone Age life. The scheme was organised by an overseas aid group wanting to bridge the gap between Papua New Guinean and Western culture. I joined up and went. With a local host, I stayed on the coast of West New Britain, with people who still wore leaf clothes, lived in grass houses and told creation stories around the fires at night-time. It was scary and I was often way out of my depth, but it was also a beautiful time. On the journey home, ill with dysentery and still culture-shocked, I stayed at a coastal airstrip with an Australian man called Marcus, a patrol officer aged about 35. Although I didn't know it at the time, Marcus was one of the people on that trip who represented the helper or mentor of the initiatory journey. While I waited for the floodwaters to recede from the airstrip and a plane to take me home, I filled in the time talking with him about life. We sat each night looking out at the Bismarck Sea, listening to the waves on the black sand beach and the deep-voiced chanting from fishermen in passing canoes.

One night he told me about his own childhood on a farm near Wilsons Promontory in Victoria. He recalled how one hot afternoon his father had received a telegram informing him that his own father had died. Marcus watched while his father ate his meal quietly and then set off into the bush at dusk. Marcus, still just a little boy, followed him at a distance, mesmerised. He found his father sitting on a hilltop overlooking the beautiful wide horizons of Corner Inlet, playing a long and mournful dirge on a harmonica. He had never heard his father play this instrument before. After listening for a time, and fearful of being discovered, he left and snuck back home.

In Port Moresby, on the way back to Australia, I realised I had no gifts for my parents, so I sold my air ticket for the Brisbane–Melbourne leg of the trip to raise funds, and bought some local artefacts. This meant I had to hitchhike the last thousand miles home (an adventure in itself). A week later, at about 2 a.m., I found myself at a highway phone booth on a deserted road about 20 miles from home. I experienced a curious impulse not to go home at all, but just to keep travelling. In the event, my tired, hungry self phoned my long-suffering parents to rescue me. But my inner self has been travelling ever since. Like many of my generation, I'm still on the road.

Perhaps you too have made such a journey, away from all that is familiar, and come back as a changed self, or perhaps there is one you need to make.

In older times, these initiatory, transitioning journeys were properly organised. People knew what they were doing. Native American young men would travel to a mountain-top and fast for days, awaiting their vision dream. In the forest below stealthy watchers guarded them from pumas and other dangers. The young people of the old cultures were too loved and too valuable to be endangered needlessly.

A friend of mine, who teaches rock climbing to young offenders and business executives, explained to me that in this apparently dangerous activity the safety is total. It isn't through pointless danger that we grow, but through the utmost care and trust in each other. When young men steal cars or run wild they are trying to recapture this process, but no mentors are there to guide them. The results fill our newspapers every day.

What are the elements of a good initiation?

The elements of initiation were remarkably consistent across many cultures. First there is a clean break from the parents, after which the boy goes to the forest, desert or wilderness. The second element is a wound that the older men give the boy, which could be a scarring of the skin, a cut with a knife, a brushing with nettles, a tooth knocked out.

The old initiators took the boys into the forest or the desert to give them a great prize – to teach them that they themselves were sacred beings. By sacred we might mean several things: that their life was part of a larger whole; that they did not live for themselves alone, but had a role to fulfil (caring for others, protection of the weak, care of natural resources); that they were no longer children – there were new privileges but also constraints. That's what initiation means. There was fear involved, and symbolic wounding, but this was done with great care and for important reasons. It was never done sadistically. The masks, dancing, rituals, magical teaching and adoption of totems gave the young man a strong sense of belonging and honour.

A Christian missionary in Uganda in the 1970s observed that certain of the young men in his college were thin and unhealthy, they lacked confidence, did not take wives and lived very poorly. He discovered that these were the ones who, through circumstance, illness or travel, had missed out on initiation. Their lives just seemed stalled.

The attention young men received at initiation was simply an intensification of the continuous involvement that uncles, grandfathers, cousins and older siblings took with boys and young men to convey to them living skills, male spirit and ways of doing things. None of these cultures would dream of leaving masculine development to chance in the way that we do.

In a magnificent essay called 'The Age of Endarkenment', the journalist Michael Ventura speaks of adolescent wildness and its challenge to our lack of ideas. Adolescents' music, fashions, words and codes, he says, announce that the initiatory moment has come. Those extravagances are a request for a response.

> Tribal people everywhere greeted the onset of
> puberty, especially in males, with elaborate and
> excruciating initiations – a practice that
> wouldn't have been necessary unless their young
> were as extreme as ours... The tribal adults didn't
> run from this moment in their children as we do;
> they celebrated it. They would assault their
> adolescents with, quite literally, holy terror;
> rituals that had been kept secret from the young
> until that moment...rituals that focused upon the
> young all the light and darkness of the tribe's
> collective psyche, all its sense of mystery, all its
> questions and all the stories told to both harbour

and answer those questions... The crucial word here is 'focus'. The adults had something to teach, stories, skills, magic, dances, visions, rituals. In fact, if these things were not learned well and completely, the tribe could not survive... Tribal cultures satisfied the craving while supplying the need, and we call that 'initiation'. This practice was so effective that usually by the age of 15 a tribal youth was able to take his or her place as a fully responsible adult.

Initiation involves more than just hanging out with the older men. The best of the culture has to be transmitted deliberately by the old men to the young. My schoolfriend whose suicide I described at the start of this book was a science nut, deeply cynical, and proud of his atheism. The science of the 1960s was very mechanical, just atoms and molecules, and saw people as little more than rats. Soon after this the death dance of the Vietnam War stirred up a fertile and life-celebrating counterculture in response. But back then we received no wisdom, no ritual, no charge with a purpose in living: there was no sense of the sacred in our high school lives. We just shambled into adulthood. In my friend's case, this lack was fatal.

Designing initiation today

There are many threshold events in the lives of young people that have aspects of initiation, and could, if we chose, be made more special and helpful in giving them a good start. For boys, owning a car and/or getting a driving licence is a significant step. A licence means that mobility and participation in the adult world are suddenly possible. A car brings independence and a greatly boosted sex life. One is also suddenly able to endanger one's own and other people's lives, so there's a massive jump in responsibility, too.

A policeman I know took his son to get his driving licence, and then drove him to the morgue. He explained gently what he intended to do, and the boy, very nervous, nonetheless consented. The two of them then went and quietly looked at some of the dead bodies stored in the cold room. The father wanted the boy, without hysteria, but with full solemnity, to know that death was real.

Some families prefer a little less intensity, but it's worth having a meal and inviting uncles and aunts – not the young man's friends, but his elders – to celebrate this rite of passage to driverhood.

Other thresholds include the first date, the final school exams, the first job. They, too, merit celebration and support. Puberty markers, such as a bar mitzvah, call out for creative celebration and adult support.

Having one's own flat, surviving away from Mum's apron strings, feeding oneself and paying the rent are important things to experience. Young men who go from Mum to wife without a self-sufficient phase between always lack a certain something, like the uninitiated

Ugandan men mentioned earlier. Make sure that your son learns to look after himself, well away from your fridge and washing machine, when the time seems right.

The wound

> Where a man's wound is, that is where his genius will be.

> **Mircea Eliade**

There is an ingredient of initiation that puzzles many people. This is the concept of the wound. Why the need for hurting? The wound has multiple meanings. Boys get wounded anyway, in body and soul, in a hundred different ways. Ritual injury is used to cleanse all preceding injuries and make them heroic instead of tragic. Just as children suffering mental anguish will sometimes burn or cut themselves to distract them from the inner pain, so those inflicting ritual pain seek to erase and make special the previous experience. There's no doubt that this is a dangerous idea, easily misused. I am ambivalent about even including it in this book. Female genital mutilation and circumcision of males are rituals that have gone too far; they damage more than they give back. More warlike and violent societies have the most harsh initiations. Our own military forces often have these, and they are frequently dehumanising and destructive. We must search for a middle path, that is a courage-proving and memorable experience, not a damaging one.

In attempting to explain why initiation in so many parts of the world involves physical pain, Robert Bly reminds us of the inner process teenage boys are inflicting on themselves: 'Early adolescence is the time traditionally chosen for initiation to begin, and we all recall how many injuries we received at that age. Adolescence is the time of risk for boys, and that risk-taking is also a yearning for initiation. Something in the adolescent male wants risk, courts danger, goes out to the edge, even to the edge of death.'

Everyone knows this tendency of boys to take risks and seek heroism. It makes sense to formalise (and therefore make safer) this craving for physical intensity as a mark of crossing a threshold. Perhaps the best equivalents we have are the well-conducted and intense outdoor experiences such as Outward Bound courses. The danger is that these may become like summer camp – a commodity you buy for your children, carried out by jaded strangers. Real initiation involves the adults who care about this child, community members who are committing themselves long term to their well-being and welcoming them into the circle of adults. (This is explored more fully in my book *Raising Boys*.)

An initiation he needed like a hole in the head

A man who was shot through the skull with an arrow by a friend trying to knock a fuel can off his head survived with no brain damage. Surgeons removed the arrow from Mr Anthony Roberts' head by drilling a larger hole around the tip at the skull's back, and pulling it through. Mr Roberts was shot on Saturday at the friend's home in Grant's Pass, about 320 km south of Portland, Oregon. Mr Roberts, an unemployed carpenter, lost his right eye. At a hospital news conference, Mr Roberts initially told reporters he was walking though a park when he heard a bow fired and then felt the arrow hit. Later he told them his friend was trying to knock the gallon can off his head as part of an initiation into a rafting and outdoor group called Mountain Men Anonymous.

Investigators said there was no doubt the can story was true. Mr Roberts said he was drinking with friends when the accident occurred. 'I don't think that's a good initiation,' he said. 'I think a hug would be better.'

If the arrow had been an inch closer to his nose, it would have severed major blood vessels, and Mr Roberts could have died on the spot. Dr Delashaw said, 'I've never seen anything like it.'

'I feel really stupid,' Mr Roberts said.

The wound turns to gold

If your life has been full of difficulty and damage, you have only two choices. You can either stay caught in the suffering, a victim for always; or you can turn it into something special, which involves making a journey through the suffering and out the other side.

> If you want to change the way you are with your sons, and your daughters, then my experience is you need to feel how you were hurt, and how you were wounded.
>
> **Marvin Allen**

We know that the greatest artists, the really great leaders, did not have cosy suburban lives. They suffered, and somehow they used the intensity of their suffering to create something transcendent and good.

The creative transformation of pain is everywhere around us, making lives interesting and worthwhile. A close friend of mine is a calm, softly spoken professional and a family man. He grew up with a father who was quite the opposite – erratic and moody, prone to outbursts of sudden violence. My friend recalls being about eight years old and his father asking him to come on a trip. The boy was scared, hid behind his mother's skirts and did not want to go. While the father yelled and stormed about the house in a rage, the boy ran to his bedroom and got into bed. Moments later the father burst into the room, lifted the whole bed and upturned it on top of the boy, who was then trapped beneath it on the floor.

When the boy grew up he became a career-driven achiever, yet never felt really happy. Only with the onset of mid-life did the pain of these experiences begin to catch up with him. He began experiencing all kinds of alarming physical reactions, such as panic attacks and sensory distortions, but luckily did not over-react or take medication. Through talking over the experiences, he made the link with his childhood and accessed many memories that had been pushed away as too painful. In time, and with help, he became more at ease with himself, able to take better care of himself and emotionally more peaceful. He also made major career changes, took a long holiday with his family, and set about a very different rhythm of life based on fulfilment rather than external achievement.

> *The father burst into the room, lifted the whole bed and upturned it on top of the boy.*

The experience of initiation

Charles Perkins is one of Australia's best-known indigenous men. A graduate in psychology and anthropology, holder of the Order of Australia, and one-time head of the Department of Aboriginal Affairs, he was the leading figure in Aboriginal politics during the 1980s.

In 1990 Perkins did a remarkable thing. He became formally initiated as a man of the Arunta people, the clan into which he was born and from which he was stolen by welfare authorities as a child. It began quite simply, when an elder confronted him late one night at a campfire meeting in the desert. The old man gave Perkins a tirade about his life and achievements, ending with a simple statement of fact: 'There's another world you don't know properly.' Perkins realised the old man was right and that he did not understand the very thing he was fighting for. He was not a real Aborigine, because he had not undergone the process of becoming one. Perkins accepted the invitation. Here, in his own words, he describes the effect on him of this experience:

> It is beyond, I think, your imagination. I could never tell anyone, explain what it means; it's just too much and nobody knows but me and the people in the ceremonies what happened and what it all means. It just boggles the mind, it really does.
>
> There are two worlds...
>
> You sit there at night, with the fires burning and maybe 200 people dancing. It was awe-inspiring... You're going back 50,000 years in time. It writes new chapters in your brain.

It was not just a personal transformation. Perkins believed that initiation, a sense of belonging, held the key to the rehabilitation of Aboriginal people, away from spiralling poverty, drunkenness and violence. Of his life before initiation, he was quoted as saying he often felt he was watching life, rather than living it:

> Unless you drink the water, or suck a few leaves, or kick a stone, or smell the flowers, you might as well be living in a movie. When I went through the ceremonies, the world changed. The trees were different, the leaves were different, the grass was different, the hills were different, the air was different. I am looking at a tree and one day it is a tree and the next day it was my friend. I saw somebody else there. I was at home.

Meeting the wild man

One way to understand the meaning of initiation is to say that it is a journey to meet the 'wild man'. The wild man is not easy to explain, although most men can in some way relate to the concept. The wild man is not savage or violent, but he is spontaneous and intuitive. He is the source of creative brilliance. He is what happens when we let go of control and trust to something inside us to do the right thing. The wild man teaches that we don't have to pretend to be good, but that we have power and integrity latent inside us, if we trust him. Abandoning yourself to wildness turns out to be the most harmonious and generative thing you can do. (Fans of Taoism and Lao Tsu will feel right at home here.) When we are good we are OK, but when we are wild we are geniuses. Any man who makes or builds things, who creates a garden, who plays a musical instrument, who has ever touched the edge of sexual ecstasy with a loving partner knows that you are better when you 'let go' and follow your impulses.

Our love of trees, the outdoors, waves and water, animals, growing things, music, children and women stems from our wild nature. The most creative men are close to the wild man and borrow his power. All masculine confidence, of the real kind, arises in the domain of the wild man. Also, the way to develop male spirituality is to know the wild man – to converse with him, not to become him. Jesus, Mohammed and Buddha were well at ease with the wild man, spending time in the wilderness, using nature as their place of prayer and reflection. All bore his hallmarks, being unpredictable and nonconformist with the established order of their times, yet at the same time disciplined and true to their inner voices. As my own minister Rod Horsfield put it, 'The truth shall make you odd.'

In her wonderful book *Women Who Run with the Wolves*, C. P. Estés recommends precisely the same to women – that they need a civilised part and a wild intuitive part, in balance. The over-civility and excessive niceness of women endangers them, just as much as it does men.

We have to learn to trust that our original nature, our inner self, is good. To be convinced of this you have only to look closely at a baby. Clearly, we are all born beautiful. This is why birth is so moving. Wordsworth was right: we come to Earth 'trailing clouds of glory'. Through initiation, we get 'hooked up' to the grid of our inborn wisdom, which knows how to breathe, how to sing, how to recognise lies, how to be brave.

We have just passed through an era when women were given the power to tell us how to be men. To be macho in any manner has become deeply unfashionable among intelligent people. And yet every man has a strong streak of machismo in his DNA. To deny it and suppress it can be deadly to men (and to the culture). Such denial can leave us depressed, without energy or passion or identity, with little to give the world. The world needs male energy that is focused, protective, exuberant and sane. It is dying from the efforts of phoney men, and from the lack of real ones.

Venus Bay – edge of the wild

Mine was a close-knit family, albeit in that buttoned-up English kind of way, and as immigrants to Australia, we became even more isolated. My sister and I were on the edge of explosive adolescence, and the family was turning into a pressure-cooker. Everyone looked forward to camping trips away from home, but wondered if we had to take each other along.

The day of our visit to Venus Bay dawned sunny and perfectly still. We had the place to ourselves and walked by the water's edge, just taking it all in. The Australian coastline still has places where the forest runs down to the sea and a sense of wild nature pervades. After we had gone a mile or so along the sea edge, I decided to go for a swim, so I walked into the trees behind the dunes for a private place to change into my swimming shorts. Standing with my clothes off, in a glade of sunlight among twisted tea trees and vines, I was aware of a combination: my body unfamiliarly naked, warm sunlight on my pale skin and the aroma of honeysuckle. There was a sense of total, primal wildness that was seductive, welcoming and mysterious all at the same time. Sexuality was in there, along with other more global feelings. At that moment I simply felt more alive than I had ever recalled feeling in my whole life. I could have run off into that forest and never returned.

This feeling of profound connection is every child's birthright. We should be able to build our life around it. All art, music, religion and poetry is an attempt to return to it. It is at the heart of what we seek in lovemaking. Yet it is the very opposite of what we build around ourselves in the modern world.

Robert Bly puts it very bluntly: 'If you are a man, civilisation will kill you.' American Indian people shared the same reaction when they saw with horror the white man's cities and towns. The Amazon people say it today. They don't so much fear the white man's world, rather they are horrified by its toxicity to a man's soul. They look at our world and pity us.

The time of Ashes

We are given a blueprint, of sorts, for the shape of a man's life. Adolescence is allowed to be rocky, then you settle down. You work and raise kids, then you retire and die. Nothing too alarming about that. But it never goes to plan. A huge and important stage that you are never told about lies in wait. It looks like bad news, but it's the complete opposite. It's the time of Ashes.

Often for men the late thirties and early forties seem to be the time of life that something goes badly wrong. Perhaps a baby is stillborn; or your wife stops loving you; or your father, sturdy and seemingly immortal, gets cancer and dies before your eyes; or you develop health problems yourself; or a car accident smashes up your body; or your career tumbles down like a pack of cards. Suddenly there is shame, error and grief all around you. Welcome to the Ashes.

The trigger for my journey downwards was a miscarriage – an abrupt end to a much-wanted pregnancy. When my partner felt the contractions after only three months of pregnancy, I swung into good husband mode. I drove us to hospital calmly and safely. I remember standing with her, my clothes soaking wet in the shower in her room at the hospital, catching in my wet hands small pieces of our hoped-for child. Still seemingly unaffected, I conducted a two-day seminar straight after the event. Then the impact came. I sank slowly into a black hole that lasted for over a year. My trademark optimism and confidence evaporated in the face of powerless grief. I became unlovable, self-absorbed, barely wanting to get out of bed. My moods served only to push away my partner, who was handling her own grief on her own timetable. I drifted towards non-being.

Somehow, gradually, as time went on, I softened inside. I was extremely confused and on unfamiliar ground, which meant a good thing started to happen. I had to swallow my pride and let friends help me, which I did not find easy. Gradually, over time, I rebuilt a sense of self that incorporated a new understanding. What I now know is that I am like everyone else – totally weak, completely vulnerable, lucky that life tests my limits so rarely, lucky just to be alive. I was, in a word, humbled. I now knew how bad other people could feel, and could have the beginnings of compassion.

You do not have to experience total devastation in order to grow into a mature man, but you have to know its possibility deep in your bones to discover that you are not all-powerful and your dreams may well not come true. Thus you make the journey down into the Ashes. If you get the message, you move on, but if you don't really go to the bottom, then it might all have to happen again. Finally you get the message, and only then do you go from being a careless boy to a more open-hearted and compassionate man.

Healing through healthy shame

An old man and a younger man are on a long camping trip across the desert. For the first few days the young man is somewhat tense and quiet. The older man notices this, but just lets it be. Finally the younger man begins to talk. He is the manager of an orchard, and in the depths of winter, just a few months previously, had backed a trailer over his own three-year-old son. Disaster was narrowly avoided because the ground was saturated and the boy was pressed down into the mud. Miraculously, he was only bruised and shocked.

The young man had been distraught for weeks. Close friends and family told him not to worry – it could have happened to anyone. He recovered somewhat, but he could not put the incident out of his mind. Even on this trip, a much-needed break, he was still experiencing flashbacks and cold sweats. The old man was silent. He did not reassure or try to minimise the feelings of the young man, who now sat silent too, feeling the familiar knotting in his gut as he once again relived the experience.

'Exactly what did people say to you?' the older man asked eventually.

'They said it was an accident. Not to blame myself. It could happen to anyone. That kind of thing.'

'Hmmm.' The old man was quiet again for a while.

'They're wrong then,' he said all of a sudden, jolting the young man from his thoughts.

'What do you mean?' he asked.

'It was a really stupid thing to do,' said the old man with almost infinite gentleness in his voice. 'You're lucky your young fella wasn't killed.'

The young man was suddenly glad it was dark around their small campfire. His face flushed and hot tears began to run down his cheeks.

'I thought my wife was looking after him. We'd just had a fight. I started the tractor. I never looked. I was thinking, it's her bloody job to keep the kids inside, and I never looked.'

By now the older man was alongside the younger one,

gripping his shoulder with one hand. The young man simply pitched forward on to the sand, wailing out loud. The older man moved alongside him and put one hand on his arm. The young man seemed to continue his curving fall into the old man's chest, holding on and sobbing in great gulps. After a time the sobbing stopped. He became aware of the warmth of the older man's shirt against his cheek, sat up a little and looked at the starry desert sky over his shoulder. A deep calmness settled into him; calmer than he had ever felt.

The grief that makes us whole

Every man needs an Ashes time in his life. To discover that, in spite of all optimism and effort, he is still vulnerable. To fall into despair at these times, though very inviting, is to miss the point. Grief is cleansing, despair is just standing still. The key is to let your feelings out.

Life is about going on, being active, making decisions, taking steps, not knowing how it will work out. Life is a tough business. If a man is able at these times to allow himself to cry and share some of his pain with his friends, he comes through a better man. He no longer looks disdainfully at poor, handicapped or weak people. He realises they are just like him. His capacity for compassion deepens enormously. The Ashes time completes what has begun in adolescence: the making of a real man.

In a nutshell

♦ Think about where you are going. What will you do when your children are gone and your wife is dead? What is your life about when there is just you?

♦ Create a space for yourself that is separate so that you can get to know yourself apart from your roles.

♦ Realise that for men, nature is where your home is. Spend time there. Pursue wildness, especially if you live in the city. Take deliberate action, such as walking on the beach, so that you can re-attune yourself to the rhythms of earth, ocean and sky.

♦ Be religious. Especially favour religions that dance, bang drums, sing or sit in total silence.

♦ Take a year off when you turn 40 and do things you have postponed or always wanted to do. Re-evaluate whether you wish to continue in the way you have been going, or make changes.

♦ Each year, around the time of your birthday, spend three days in complete solitude.

♦ Think about whether you need some kind of initiation into manhood to move from being a perpetual adolescent.

♦ Learn about the ancient culture of the land you live on.

♦ Accept times of great misfortune, such as a marriage breakdown, sickness or business failure, as essential steps to getting free. Roll in the Ashes. Don't be afraid of pain, grief, sadness, weakness or failure. They enrich your humanness.

♦ Go looking for the wild man.

Appendix:

Some Thoughts about the Importance of Male Community

I hope that reading this book has given you some good ideas for your own life, which you may already have begun to implement. But perhaps you are feeling a little overwhelmed. One problem with the whole self-help and self-improvement scene is the expectation that we can change things all on our own. Contemporary man has been plagued by this illusion. When this solitary approach fails, we conclude that nothing can be changed after all, and give up. So today many young men are brashly over-confident and most older men are depressed.

Since writing the first edition of *Manhood*, I have learnt more about the importance of having a male community. To make personal change easier, and to make global change possible, we have to build and belong to a community of men who are working towards similar goals. Small groups of men who are willing to meet regularly and talk can give each other huge insights, enormous amounts of encouragement and occasional kicks in the bum – all essential to keeping you open and moving towards liberation. If you want your life as a man really to get moving, you should consider joining or starting a men's group. Here are some guidelines.

How men's groups work

In a living room not far from where you are reading this, odds are that a group of eight or nine men meets every couple of weeks to talk about their lives. Their wives or partners are happy to vacate the house on that night because they like the results: happier, more balanced, stronger and more peaceful men.

There are thousands of men's groups in the USA. In the UK, Germany, South America, Australia and New Zealand men's groups are forming (often prompted by this book), writing newsletters, communicating on the Internet, holding conferences and getting excited. Different emphases are emerging: in the USA there are special efforts being made to bridge men of different races; in Australia good links are being forged with Aboriginal people, and there is a focus on the mentoring of adolescent boys; in Northern Ireland there is an emphasis on helping young fathers to do a better job.

The structure of a men's group is based on some key guidelines. There is no pressure to speak unless you wish to. There is an emphasis on hearing someone out, rather than interrupting with argument or well-meaning advice. (Most people get plenty of this in their normal lives.) The emphasis is also on speaking from the heart, not discussing or theorising in the abstract.

At times men's groups can be emotional. Something very freeing happens when a private space is set aside, when the rules are 'No bullshitting' and 'Say what you feel'. If men know their stories will be heard and honoured, then a great deal finds its way to the surface.

Men's groups are also very practical. The chosen topic of the night may be 'How to discipline your kids', or 'How to break out of an alienating career and make time to live'. It might be some frank discussion about sex, or it might be more crisis-driven – helping a man wounded from marital combat, or a group member whose wife has just been diagnosed with cancer. I've listened in men's groups to older men talk about war trauma, honestly, for the first time after decades of silence.

Young men find surrogate fathers and uncles in the group. Depressed older men find a reason to feel they have something to offer. The ethics of men's groups are strong, particularly about never acting (or even speaking) violently to women, children or each other. Men's group talk has a style that is very different from women's talk: there's less tiptoeing and less tendency to agree with everything you say.

Men's groups usually meet in members' homes, though occasionally they are church-based or meet in a health centre. Most are general purpose, but some are specifically for men with violence problems, or health or marital concerns. A group may close its membership once it is running, though some will invite new members periodically. The most common way to start is to invite a few friends and begin your own. Four or five men are enough; up to 12 can function well as a unit. Some groups use a book (such as this one) as a discussion starter, or generate a list of topics agreed by the members. Leadership tends to be rotated, rather than having no leader at all, acknowledging that men like structure and are goal-orientated.

Among the rules in men's groups are no put-downs and strict confidentiality. There is also a tendency to confront bullshit or irresponsibility. 'You're neglecting your goddamn kids, man! When are you going to wake up to yourself!' 'Well, sure you could leave your wife, but you'd be an idiot to do it. Why don't you talk to her and tell her what you're feeling?' 'You're tired, mate. You and your wife need a holiday.' And so on. You don't have to speak in a men's group – there isn't any pressure. Perhaps for that very reason, though, you soon find yourself sharing your life, prompted by the similarities between your own experiences and those being shared by the other men. You get practical tips for living and feel you can breathe more deeply, all at the same time. It adds a sense of relaxation to your life (very different from getting drunk or going fishing) because the changes are long lasting. Your life starts to make more sense because you are reflecting and reporting on it to interested friends.

Most men's groups reach a point where they organise to get away for weekends. In groups where most men are fathers, activities are often planned to include the youngsters. Some groups, such as YMCA Explorers, exist specifically for dads and daughters or dads and sons to spend time together, supported by some resources and structure.

Men's groups can become activist in nature, as a counterbalance to all the talk. Fred Hollows, a famous Australian eye surgeon who took his skills to the developing world, belonged to such a group. When a row of tobacco billboards was erected along his favourite stretch of coast, he went with his friends and chain-sawed them down on a dark and cloudy night. The company replaced them with steel posts a few months later. Fred's group returned with steel-cutting equipment and chopped them down again. After that the company gave up.

Where men's groups can lead

What about the big picture? Men's needs, such as paternity leave and flexible working hours, require changes in legislation and the workplace. As men wean off the earn and spend cycle, the economy and the wider world will be affected in many ways. People will consider other necessary changes, including: the way that boys are treated in schools; the access situation for separated fathers; the exploitation of young men in sport; the sexual abuse of boys; men in the military; rape in prisons; the right of children to have and know their fathers; the need we all have for wild and natural places to be preserved; the prevention of rape and harassment of women. The field is wide.

Making a world that is kinder to men will make men kinder. This is the missing piece of the social reform jigsaw. Who knows where it might take us? If you're a man, you're part of it and your actions will make a difference. If you're a woman reading this, thank you for your love and understanding.

In a nutshell

♦ The self-made man is a myth. We all need the help of others to make and sustain change.

♦ Join a men's group, or start one with friends.

♦ Groups that succeed usually have a structure or programme, and rotate leadership to keep direction and purpose. As you begin to stabilise or get bored, do something for your community. But don't ever lose the reflective aspect encouraged by the group.

♦ A planet-wide movement for men's liberation and betterment is gathering momentum. And about time!

Future Dreaming

Men in the future will...

Work less, play more.

Earn less, spend less.

Parent more, stay married longer.

Live longer.

Be safer to be around.

They will also...

Have more friends, and be closer to those friends.

Watch less sport and play more sport.

Take a long-term interest in outdoor and wilderness pursuits, of a quieter and more experiential kind.

Become quietly dedicated to, almost religious about ecological activism.

As lovers they will...

Be better in bed, more alive in their bodies.

More confident, less needy.

More friendly, in less of a hurry.

As fathers men will...

Be warm, playful, creative, involved and positive.

When they need to, they will take a firm stand, without being attacking or intimidating.

As consumers they will...

Dress more warmly and colourfully. Wear handmade and decorative but distinctively masculine clothes and artefacts. (The suit and tie will disappear. Like the top hat and the frock coat, they will become historical oddities.)

Drive old but classy cars, and look after them.

Learn to play more musical instruments.

Prefer 'world' music and move away from youth-orientated styles or products.

Admire but not envy young people. The cult of youth will disappear, and young people will be seen as they are – lovely but immature.

See old age and experience revalued in everything from fashion to films, employment trends to leadership choices.

Discover role models in their fifties and older, especially men and women of a warm and unhurried kind, who are still prickly and confronting, authoritative and humorous.

Take a greater interest in their inner world, which will lead existing religions to be revitalised. In addition, new hybrids and forms of ceremony will be evolved, especially those helping men to heal their pasts and to initiate their teenage sons. A gradual blurring of religion and ecology will begin to emerge as a power in its own right.

As individuals men will...

Make their fortieth year a sabbatical from work and pursue other goals, as a kind of ritual choice.

Use the insights they gain from their year out to decide whether to continue in their career or make changes.

Spend a few days each year, around the time of their birthday, in complete solitude.

Confront and work with child abusers, rapists and wife beaters in caring but extremely tough monitoring networks and self-help groups. This will save police resources for more white-collar crime work!

Organise themselves and work alongside women in the community, developing innovative political and activist organisations to tackle local and global issues, using myriad computer networks, faxes and newsletters.

Alter the face of schools, rewrite the whole nature of childhood, wrest local councils back from business interests, demolish traditional political parties, and work and network with developing countries and indigenous people to learn from them more about how to live, love and heal on this planet.

Bibliography

Books quoted in the text

BLANKENHORN, DAVID Fatherless America, Basic Books, New York, 1995.

BLY, ROBERT Iron John: A Book About Men, Element, London, 1991.

DALBEY, GORDON Healing the Masculine Soul, Word, Melbourne, 1989.

ELIUM, DON AND JEANNE Raising a Son, Beyond Words, California, 1992.

EMBLING, JOHN Fragmented Lives: A darker side of Australian life, Penguin, Melbourne, 1986.

GOLDBERG, HERB The New Male, Bantam, New York, 1984.

HAGAN, KAY LEIGH (editor) Women Respond to the Men's Movement, Pandora/HarperCollins, San Francisco, 1993.

HARDING, CHRISTOPHER (editor) Wingspan – Inside the Men's Movement, St Martins Press, New York, 1992.

HENDERSON, JULIE The Lover Within, Station Hill Press, UK, 1995.

JONES, CAROLINE The Search for Meaning (3), ABC/Collins Dove, Sydney, 1992.

KEEN, SAM Fire in the Belly, Bantam, New York, 1992.

LEE, JOHN At My Father's Wedding, Bantam, New York, 1991.

MIEDZIAN, MYRIAM Boys Will Be Boys, Virago, London, 1992.

RHODES, RICHARD Making Love, Simon & Schuster, New York, 1992.

SCHNARCH, DAVID Passionate Marriage, Norton, UK, 1997

THOMPSON, KEITH (editor) To Be a Man: In Search of the Deep Masculine, Jeremy Tarcher, Los Angeles, 1991.

Articles quoted in the text

ALLEN, MARVIN from the documentary 'Wild Man Weekend', SBS Television.

ASSOCIATED PRESS 'An initiation he needed like a hole in the head', The Mercury.

BALDWIN, JAMES quoted in To Be a Man (Christopher Harding).

BLISS, SHEPHERD cited in Wingspan (Christopher Harding).

BLY, ROBERT Bloomsbury Review, January, 1991.

CAMUS, ALBERT quoted in To Be a Man (Keith Thompson).

COONEY, BARRY 'Touching the Masculine Soul', in Wingspan (Christopher Harding).

FEINLEIN, PROF. WALKER p.comm. over counter-lunch at the Black Buffalo Hotel, North Hobart.

FOLLET, KEN from Night Over Water, quoted by Barry Oakley, the Australian Magazine.

FRIEDAN, BETTY 'The Second Stage', 1981, cited in Wingspan (Christopher Harding).

GILLETTE, DOUGLAS 'Men and Intimacy', in Wingspan (Christopher Harding).

HARDING, CHRIS 'Men's Secret Societies, 1890s-1990s', in Wingspan (Christopher Harding).

HAYWARD, FREDRIC 'Male Bashing', originally appeared in To Be a Man (Keith Thompson).

KABIR quoted in Iron John (Robert Bly).

LAWRENCE, D.H. Women in Love, quoted by Barry Oakley in the Australian Magazine.

LAWRENCE, D.H. 'Healing', from The Complete Poems of D.H. Lawrence, quoted in Iron John (Robert Bly).

LEUNIG, MICHAEL 'The Demon', from A Bunch of Poesy, Angus & Robertson/HarperCollins, Sydney, 1992.

LEUNIG, MICHAEL interviewed by Caroline Jones in The Search for Meaning (3).

MASTERS, ROBERT 'Ditching the Bewitching Myth', in To Be a Man (Keith Thompson).

NOA, JAI 'The Cripple and the Man', in Baumli, F., (editor) Men Freeing Men, New Atlantis Press, 1985.

PERKINS, CHARLES quoted by Stuart Rintoul in the Australian, 15 February, 1992.

RINTOUL, STUART 'Initiation', in the Australian, 15 Feb, 1992.

SIMENON, GEORGES quoted in Wingspan (Christopher Harding).

TAYLOR, GEORGE 'Longing for the Great Father', in Wingspan (Christopher Harding).

VENTURA, MICHAEL 'Shadowdancing', quoted in Wingspan (Christopher Harding).

Videos

BLY, ROBERT (WITH BILL MOYERS) 'A Gathering of Men', PBS Television.

ALLEN, MARVIN 'Wild Man Weekend', SBS Television.

Contacts and Resources

The following contacts are included as a useful starting point for those wishing to make contact with organisations working with men and with men's groups.

NAVIGATOR
Men's Development Programme
James Traeger, Jenny Daisley and Liz Willis
The Springboard Consultancy, P.O. Box 69
Stroud, Glos. GL5 5EE
Tel: 01453 787540   Fax: 01453 872363
E-mail: springboard@compuserve.com
www.springboardconsultancy.com
Navigator is a personal development programme for men geared to improving personal effectiveness in the workplace.

Achilles Heel: The Radical Men's Magazine
4 West Park Villas
Horrabridge, Devon PL20 7TY
Tel: 01822 853 165
www.stejonda.demon.co.uk/achilles
To subscribe to the magazine, write to Achilles Heel Subscriptions at the above address. The website contains selected articles, book reviews and links.

The Centre for Men's Development
154 Stoke Newington Church Street
London N16 0JU
Tel: 020 7686 1293 Fax: 020 7607 9330
E-mail: headexchange@gn.apc.org

Company of Men
c/o Martin Kemp, 209 Conkwell, Wiltshire BA15 2JF
Tel: 01225 722006

Fathers Direct
Herald House, Lambs Passage, Bunhill Row
London EC1Y 8TQ
Tel: 020 7920 9491 Fax: 020 7374 2966
E-mail: enquiries@fathersdirect.com
www.fathersdirect.com
National think-tank and lobby group advocating the importance of
fathers. Fathers Direct publishes extensive research, DAD magazine
and Fatherwork journal for those working with fathers.

Journeyman
c/o Geoff Mead, 7 Reading Road North, Bramshill
Hook, Hants RG27 0JW
Tel: 01256 602151

Men's Databank
c/o Derek Shiel, 25 Randolph Crescent, London W9 1DP
Tel: 020 7286 1173

Men's Health Helpline
Tel: 020 8995 4448

Men for Change Network
c/o Steve Banks, 36 Beechwood Road
London N8 7NG
Tel/Fax: 020 8348 9266
National Network of men who have agreed to act as local contact
points for men looking for men's groups, or who are interested in
Menswork. To see the list of contacts, buy the latest issue of *Achilles
Heel* (see above) or write, enclosing a SAE, to Men for Change
Network.

The Men's Project
c/o Colin Fowler
Parents Advice Centre
12 Brunswick Street, Belfast BT2 7GE
Tel: (028) 90 310891
Email: colin@mensproject.org www.mensproject.org
Networking those working with men across Northern Ireland and
the Republic.

Menswork
c/o Derek Close, 2 Ashfield Cottages, Rockwood Road
Chepstow, Gwent NP6 5DU
Tel/Fax: 01291 623514

Network for a New Men's Leadership
45 Nutgrove Avenue, Bristol BS3 4QF
Tel: 0117 940 7254

Parent Network
Room 2, Winchester House, Kennington Park
11 Cranmer Road, London SW9 6EJ
Tel: 020 7735 1214
For courses on parenting.

Survivors
PO Box 2470, London W2 1NW
Tel: 020 7833 3737
Helpline for male sexual abuse.

Working With Men
320 Commercial Way, London SE15 1QN
Tel: 020 7732 9409
For professionals who work with men and boys on issues of
violence, sexism, sexual abuse and masculinity.

Websites
www.stevebiddulph.com
www.manhood.com.au
www.sievxmemorial.com
www.coeffic.demon.co.uk/organiz.htm - *keeping parents and children in contact*
www.coeffic.demon.co.uk/descrim.htm - *discrimination against men*
users.zetnet.co.uk/zeus/topics.htm – *men's health in the media*
www.stejonda.demon.co.uk/achilles/ - *Achilles Heel on line*
www.garfnet.org.uk/new_mill/dec95/carrie.htm - *men deserve education about health awareness*
www.vix.com/pub/men - *men's page index at vix.com*
www.menstuff.org - *committed to questioning society's expectations of men*
freespace.virgin.net/mens.health/ - *a charity about men's health*
www.prostate.org - *Prostatitis Foundation*
www.acor.org/TCRC/ - *testicular cancer research centre*

Index

Also available from Vermilion

New Toddler Taming
A parents' guide to the first four years
Dr Christopher Green

Revised and updated for the twenty-first century, *New Toddler Taming* offers friendly, practical advice for a new generation of parents with children at the challenging stage of toddlerdom, including:

- sleep solutions that really work
- successful potty training
- discipline – how to make life easier for yourself
- being a working parent
- the very latest on healthy eating

And much more!

Adolescence
A guide for parents
Michael Carr-Gregg and Erin Shale

The ultimate guide to helping your child deal with adolescence and become a confident, resilient adult. This book gives clear and concise advice with strategies parents need to guide their children through the teen years into adulthood.

Intelligent Memory
Exercise your mind and make yourself smarter
Dr Barry Gordon

Memory is not just our brain's databank – much more important is intelligent memory, the system that allows us to have ideas, insight and creativity. The good news is that it is not fixed at birth, but strengthens with age, and is exceptionally malleable. Dr Gordon explains how to expand it, which he compares to learning to drive: slow at first, but getting fast, accurate and unconscious with practice.

The Money Diet
The ultimate guide to shedding pounds off your bills and saving money on everything!
Martin Lewis

Want to save thousands of pounds?
Just follow this simple diet.

The average person spends more money on their telephone bill than stocks and shares, so why do finance books always talk about the markets? Whether it's utilities, credit cards, DVDs or debt, *The Money Diet* holds the secret of how to get more money in your pocket. With crash diet tips for speedy savings, a healthy eating guide to debt management and a complete financial fitness programme, Martin Lewis could save you up to £6,000 a year with his easy to implement, cutting-edge advice.

☐ **New Toddler Taming**	0091875285	£12.99
☐ **Adolescence**	0091891620	£8.99
☐ **Intelligent Memory**	0091884241	£10.99
☐ **The Money Diet**	0091894840	£7.99

FREE POSTAGE AND PACKING

Overseas customers allow £2.00 per paperback

BY PHONE: 01624 677237

BY POST: Random House Books
C/o Bookpost, PO Box 29, Douglas
Isle of Man, IM99 1BQ

BY FAX: 01624 670923

BY EMAIL: bookshop@enterprise.net

Cheques (payable to Bookpost) and credit cards accepted

Prices and availability subject to change without notice.
Allow 28 days for delivery.
When placing your order, please mention if you do not wish
to receive any additional information.

www.randomhouse.co.uk